10+

j.john

Ten Service Outlines
for church leaders
based on
the Ten Commandments

MONARCH
BOOKS

Mill Hill, London NW7 3SA and Grand Rapids, Michigan 49501

First published by Monarch Books in the UK in 2001,
Concorde House, Grenville Place, Mill Hill, London NW7 3SA.
Published in the USA by Monarch Books 2001.
Distributed by:
UK: STL, PO Box 300, Kingstown Broadway,
Carlisle, Cumbria CA3 0QS;
USA: Kregel Publications, PO Box 2607,
Grand Rapids, Michigan 49501.

ISBN 1 85424 514 7 (UK)
ISBN 0 8254 6015 8 (USA)

British Library Cataloguing Data
A catalogue record for this book is available
from the British Library.

Book design and production for the publisher by
Gazelle Creative Productions,
Concorde House, Grenville Place, Mill Hill, London NW7 3SA.

CONTENTS

*'Wise speech is rarer and more valuable than
gold and rubies.'*
Proverbs 20:15

*It wasn't raining when
Noah built the ark.*

*'It usually takes me more than
three weeks to prepare a good impromptu speech.'*
– Mark Twain

INTRODUCTION

Over the last few years I have been travelling around the UK doing sequences of ten talks on the Ten Commandments. The interest shown has astonished me. To have people come to a one-off event is one thing but to have them turn out – sometimes in their thousands – week after week is another. Plainly, the commandments and the whole issue of how we should live are issues high on the life agenda of people today.

But all the talking that I have done has really only just scratched the surface of the hunger for teaching in this area. And I have my limitations; I can't personally do a ten-week series at every town hall and church from Land's End to John O'Groats. Hence this book; in it I have tried to supply the resources for people in local churches to do something themselves on the Ten Commandments.

In this book there are ten service outlines based upon each of the commandments. The first thing to say about these outlines is that they are designed with a variety of churches in mind. I know my church and I know what works with me; obviously I do not know the chemistry generated between you and your church. You could, I suppose, just take these outlines and use them 'cold' as a sort of 'just-add-water' service package. But that is not the best use. This material is designed as a framework for you to look at, think about, pray over and modify as you see fit.

You will see as soon as you turn to the first service that I am treating the commandments in reverse order, starting with the Tenth Commandment. This is an order that I have used elsewhere and there is logic rather than perversity behind it. The commandments were originally given to a people who were already committed to God, who knew something of him and who were well aware of the issues involved in following him. Accordingly, in the sequence that they are given in the Bible, the commandments start with the basis of the covenant ('Worship only the Lord') and gradually work outwards through the implications of that commitment. I feel, however, that with the limited knowledge of the Bible and God among today's generation is it easier to start with coveting and move inwards towards the First Commandment. By then its demands for a wholehearted and exclusive devotion to God may make more sense. Now if you disagree, fine. Of course the services can be switched around but do bear in mind that they have been written with this inwards trend in mind.

LAYOUT OF SERVICES

Each service includes the following:

- **Suggested hymns and songs**
- **Warm-up activity to get people involved**
- **Children's activity**
- **Bible readings**
- **Poem by Stewart Henderson**
- **Sermon**
- **Suggested prayers**

Let me briefly discuss these activities in detail.

1) SUGGESTED HYMNS AND SONGS
These hymns and songs are merely a few that are possible. I am grateful to Matt Redman for suggesting which of his songs would be suitable and making other recommendations. Many of the hymns and some of the other songs were identified from the

excellent *Hymnquest 2000* CD-ROM (see www.hymnquest.com). With many of the older hymns do bear in mind that a reworking into a more accessible modern English language may exist (probably in a *Jubilate Hymns* version).

There are few hymns or songs (of any era) specifically written about the Ten Commandments. However, many hymns or songs in worship books under the categories of 'Confession', 'Repentance', 'Commitment' or 'Dedication' may be suitable. It is probably sensible, theologically and musically, to match some of the minor-key confessional hymns and songs with more major-key praise hymns and songs that affirm the goodness of God. The issue of coveting for example is not simply that it is bad; it is that our desires should be aimed towards Christ instead. The hymns and songs suggested try to reflect this.

2) WARM-UP ACTIVITY TO GET PEOPLE INVOLVED
These start-up activities are designed to make people interested and to get them involved from the very beginning. The danger of people coming into a church and immediately letting their minds slide into neutral cannot be underestimated. An activity or a question-and-answer session like this can, if it works well, have people riveted. Even where the activity doesn't work as well as you would like, you will have at least established that you are trying to communicate and are not simply performing for your own amusement.

3) CHILDREN'S ACTIVITY
I have tried to put something in to keep the attention of younger members of the congregation. Actually in most cases the children's activity has a secondary goal of making a relevant point to the rest of the congregation. Frequently you will find that the sermon alludes to the activity carried out with the children.

4) BIBLE READINGS
For each of the commandments I have selected several passages of Scripture. These have been laid out for dramatic reading using

a small number of people for the performance. The Bible version used here is the New Living Translation; its clarity of expression, natural and lively language lend itself well for this purpose. In almost every case I have followed the text exactly; the only omissions are of redundant phrases like 'And he said'. I have put a cast list at the start of each reading so that you know what type of character is needed.

Occasionally I have appended comments on the voice required. In most cases these are obvious, but do remember that the wrong voice can negate the strongest text. Some voices such as Introducer, Text Narrator, Voice of the LORD, etc. occur repeatedly and some general comments are given where they first occur (mostly in Service One).

5) POEM BY STEWART HENDERSON

My friend Stewart Henderson has written a series of ten poems articulating a contemporary response to each commandment. These poems can be used at any appropriate point in the service.

Here's a taster of the whole ten:

> *Why have them? These killjoys,*
> *this 'Thou Shalt Not' list.*
> *The more we ignore them,*
> *the less they'll be missed.*

> **To some they're restrictive,**
> **a chain on the soul.**
> **Despotic religion's**
> **oppressive control.**
> **Iron handed, mean minded,**
> **a rod for the back.**
> **Stifling decrees**
> **in Victorian black.**

Why have them? These killjoys,
this 'Thou Shalt Not' list.
The more we ignore them,
the less they'll be missed.

To others, they're narrow,
reactionary rules.
Inflexible laws
to be phased out of schools.
Obsolete maxims,
old fashioned ways.
Negative codes
from empirical days.

For now we are cultured –
a society renewed,
with Kosovo, landmines,
laboratory food.
Ecology summits,
an anxious new dawn.
Bone marrow transplants
and Internet porn.

Why have them? These killjoys,
this 'Thou Shalt Not' list.
The more we ignore them,
the less they'll be missed.

So how should we view
such archaic advice?
Stark sermonising?
Gems without price?
Wise regulations?
A sheltering place?
A self-help directory?
A charter for grace?

Why have them? These killjoys,
this 'Thou Shalt Not' list.
The more we ignore them,
the less they'll be missed.

6) SERMON

I started by calling these a 'sermon/talk' but the term looked so awkward I just left it as 'sermon'. What you choose to call your talk is of course your own decision.

Let me first say what I have not done here. I have not simply repeated the sort of thing that I would say in my talks. There are several reasons for this. First, what works for me may well not work for you. Secondly, what has burdened me about a commandment may not be where your own heart lies.

So what I have done for each commandment is to produce a general sermon on what I think are the main implications of that commandment for today's lifestyle. You may well wish to branch off onto a particular emphasis of your own or omit some of the material; I just felt it important to try to map out as much of the ground as accurately as I could. The result is, I am aware, a rather bland flavour. That is deliberate; it is easier to add flavouring than to take it out.

While I have put in some illustrations, they are the sort of thing that I think you are best able to do yourself. You know the sort of illustration that will work with your listeners better than I do. In some places I have put in comments that I think may be worth considering when you are preparing the material.

7) SUGGESTED PRAYERS

The words given here are merely suggestions based on my own reflections of these commandments. I suggest that you add or modify these according to your church setting.

AND FINALLY...

Please remember two things.

First, these services are meant to have a practical impact. God did not give the commandments (or anything else in the Bible) for us to produce nothing more than beautiful worship experiences and eloquent sermons. These commandments make demands in the real world of work and relationships. How exactly the commandments are to be applied in our personal lives requires thought and prayer. A great help in this respect are small group Bible studies where people are forced to grapple with what the Word of God is saying to them. Written parallel to this book is *Ten Plus Study Guide: a group study of the Ten Commandments in ten or twenty sessions.*

Secondly, the fact that these services are meant to have a practical impact means that they may disturb and even hurt. By talking about these commandments you will be touching on things close to our lives; parents, children, spouses, anger, frustration. Tread sensitively, gently and lovingly and be prepared for God's Spirit to work in lives.

Finally, I pray that you and those involved in taking part in these services will be richly blessed by using this material.

Don't Covet!

Commandment 10: Exodus 20:17 'Do not covet your neigh-bour's house. Do not covet your neighbour's wife, male or female servant, ox or donkey, or anything else your neighbour owns.'

1) SUGGESTED HYMNS AND SONGS

HYMNS

- Christ whose glory fills the skies
- Be thou my vision O Lord of my heart
- When I survey the wondrous cross
- Ye holy angels bright
- Thou didst leave thy throne and thy kingly crown
- Jesus I have promised

SONGS

- Take the world but give me Jesus [Matt Redman]
- Abba, Father let me be
- When I look into your holiness
- Reign in me, Sovereign Lord

2) WARM-UP ACTIVITIES AND ILLUSTRATIONS

These are designed to get people thinking.

SHOPPING LIST

Have a pad of paper and go round asking people what they would like someone to buy them. Encourage them to come up with ideas, however lavish. Very soon you will have a very long and very expensive list.

ADVERTISEMENTS

Questions. Ask:

- What are people's favourite adverts? Why?
- Why do adverts work?

[Note: The answer you want to draw out is that they encourage us to think we need their product to live a good quality of life.]

Point out that our desires are being shaped by the world around us – what we need is to have our desires shaped by God.

QUOTABLE FIGURES

- By the time we are 35 we have seen 150,000 TV commercials, 75,000 minutes or two months of your entire life
- An average £82 million is spent each week on the lottery – the odds on winning are 13, 983, 816 to 1
- 90% of those who win the lottery jackpot keep playing
- 70% of 18–24 year olds define future success in terms of wealth and career
- At the beginning of the year 2000 the world's 3 richest people had more money than half of the 47 poorest countries, and 342 people had more money than half the world's population

3) CHILDREN'S ACTIVITY

PREPARATION

- Get a strong cardboard box and make a small hole in a side just wide enough for a child's hand to get in. Reinforce the edges so it cannot be bent under pressure. Seal the box.

- Get two chocolate eggs. One is the small inch-long variety while the other is the hen's-egg-sized cream-filled type.

ACTIVITY
- Display the large chocolate egg and push it in through the hole in the box. It will fit through easily.
- Pick on someone and ask them to make a decision; they can either have the small egg or the large egg; but not both.
- The volunteer will probably want to try for the larger egg.
- If the hole has been cut to the right size then although they can grasp the egg with their hands they will not be able to withdraw their hand while still holding it.

CONCLUSION
Point out that the volunteer has got himself or herself trapped. They can pull their hand out but only by leaving the egg inside. And if they do that they will lose that egg and the little one they could have had.

Wanting something we are not supposed to have is called coveting. It is a bit like being greedy. Coveting causes lots of problems. Often because they want something they can't have, people get involved in things that are hard to get out of. They may borrow money that they can't repay or they may lose friends. But they are never happy because they always want more. They often fail to get something larger and in the process lose the little they have.

God wants us to be happy. But coveting things never satisfies. We need to learn to be satisfied with what God has given us. And to thank him.

Now give the volunteer both eggs as a reward.

4) BIBLE READINGS

OLD TESTAMENT
I suggest two readings; one of two possible psalms and the tale from 1 Kings 21 about Naboth's vineyard.

Psalms

Suggest either: Psalm 37:1–7 or Psalm 145.

CAST
Reader: These passages will probably work best with a single good reader

Psalm 37:1–7

    Don't worry about the wicked.
    Don't envy those who do wrong.
    For like grass, they soon fade away.
    Like springtime flowers, they soon wither.
    Trust in the Lord and do good.
    Then you will live safely in the land and prosper.
    Take delight in the Lord,
    and he will give you your heart's desires.
    Commit everything you do to the Lord.
    Trust him, and he will help you.
    He will make your innocence as clear as the dawn,
    and the justice of your cause will shine like the noonday
        sun.
    Be still in the presence of the Lord,
    and wait patiently for him to act.
    Don't worry about evil people who prosper
    or fret about their wicked schemes.

or

Psalm 145

    I will praise you, my God and King,
    and bless your name forever and ever.
    I will bless you every day,
    and I will praise you forever.
    Great is the LORD! He is most worthy of praise!
    His greatness is beyond discovery!
    Let each generation tell its children

of your mighty acts.
I will meditate on your majestic, glorious splendour
and your wonderful miracles.
Your awe-inspiring deeds will be on every tongue;
I will proclaim your greatness.
Everyone will share the story of your wonderful goodness;
they will sing with joy of your righteousness.
The LORD is kind and merciful,
slow to get angry, full of unfailing love.
The LORD is good to everyone.
He showers compassion on all his creation.
All of your works will thank you, LORD,
and your faithful followers will bless you.
They will talk together about the glory of your kingdom;
they will celebrate examples of your power.
They will tell about your mighty deeds
and about the majesty and glory of your reign.
For your kingdom is an everlasting kingdom.
You rule generation after generation.
The LORD is faithful in all he says;
he is gracious in all he does.
The LORD helps the fallen and lifts up those bent beneath
    their loads.
All eyes look to you for help;
you give them their food as they need it.
When you open your hand,
you satisfy the hunger and thirst of every living thing.
The LORD is righteous in everything he does;
he is filled with kindness.
The LORD is close to all who call on him,
yes, to all who call on him sincerely.
He fulfills the desires of those who fear him;
he hears their cries for help and rescues them.
The LORD protects all those who love him,
but he destroys the wicked.
I will praise the LORD,

and everyone on earth will bless his holy name
forever and forever.

1 Kings 21:1-24

CAST

Introducer: It should be plain here and elsewhere from the tone of voice and manner that what the Introducer says is not Scripture. He or she could be placed slightly oblique or offset to the other characters.

Text Narrator: Here and elsewhere the Text Narrator should have a matter-of-fact voice.

King Ahab: Should sound thoroughly spoilt

Naboth: Has only one line to speak but it must be done with utter integrity

Jezebel: Merciless and ruthless

The LORD: This is a difficult one to bring off. While a faltering treble whisper for the voice of the LORD is not appropriate, an over-theatrical booming bass may invite ridicule. One possibility is for the LORD to speak from 'off-stage' with an amplified and slightly over-reverberant voice.

Elijah: Hard, no-nonsense, authoritative

Introducer: There are few more innocent things in life than wanting a vegetable garden. After all what harm can come from the desire for a few vines, the odd line of beans and some prize marrows? But, as King Ahab of Israel found out, some desires are wrong and can lead to disaster.

After the death of Solomon, the Jewish nation split into two parts; a northern kingdom of Israel and a southern kingdom of Judah. Ahab was the seventh king of Israel and ruled for twenty years in the middle of the ninth century BC. He was a talented diplomat, a successful leader in battle and a ruler who brought prosperity to his land. He could have been a great king and have founded a dynasty.

But instead his reign and his entire family line came to a bloody and terrible end.

In Israel the powers of a king were limited by the law of God. For instance you couldn't just take a piece of land. The land was a gift from the LORD to a family forever. It could be rented but not sold; not even to a king. But Ahab's wife Jezebel had been the daughter of the King of Sidon, and there kings were really kings and when they wanted something they took it.

Text Narrator: King Ahab had a palace in Jezreel, and near the palace was a vineyard owned by a man named Naboth. One day Ahab said to Naboth…

Ahab: Since your vineyard is so convenient to the palace, I would like to buy it to use as a vegetable garden. I will give you a better vineyard in exchange, or if you prefer, I will pay you for it.

Naboth: The LORD forbid that I should give you the inheritance that was passed down by my ancestors.

Text Narrator: So Ahab went home angry and sullen because of Naboth's answer. The king went to bed with his face to the wall and refused to eat! His wife, Jezebel, asked him…

Jezebel: What in the world is the matter? What has made you so upset that you are not eating?

Ahab: I asked Naboth to sell me his vineyard or to trade it, and he refused!

Jezebel: Are you the king of Israel or not? Get up and eat and don't worry about it. I'll get you Naboth's vineyard!

Text Narrator: So she wrote letters in Ahab's name, sealed them with his seal, and sent them to the elders and other leaders of the city where Naboth lived. In her letters she commanded:

Jezebel: Call the citizens together for fasting and prayer and give Naboth a place of honour. Find two scoundrels who will accuse him of cursing God and the king. Then take him out and stone him to death.

Text Narrator: So the elders and other leaders followed the instructions Jezebel had written in the letters. They called for a fast and put Naboth at a prominent place before the people. Then two scoundrels accused him before all the people of cursing God and the king. So he was dragged outside the city and stoned to death. The city officials then sent word to Jezebel, 'Naboth has been stoned to death.' When Jezebel heard the news, she said to Ahab...

Jezebel: You know the vineyard Naboth wouldn't sell you? Well, you can have it now! He's dead!

Text Narrator: So Ahab immediately went down to the vineyard to claim it. But the LORD said to Elijah, who was from Tishbe...

The LORD: Go down to meet King Ahab, who rules in Samaria. He will be at Naboth's vineyard in Jezreel, taking possession of it. Give him this message: 'This is what the LORD says: Isn't killing Naboth bad enough? Must you rob him, too? Because you have done this, dogs will lick your blood outside the city just as they licked the blood of Naboth!'

Ahab: So my enemy has found me!

Elijah: Yes, I have come because you have sold yourself to what is evil in the LORD's sight. The LORD is going to bring disaster to you and sweep you away. He will not let a single one of your male descendants, slave or free alike, survive in Israel! He is going to destroy your family as he did the family of Jeroboam son of Nebat and the family of Baasha son of Ahijah, for you have made him very angry and have led all of Israel into sin. The LORD has also told me that the dogs of Jezreel will eat the body of your wife, Jezebel, at the city wall. The members of your family who die in the city will be eaten by dogs, and those who die in the field will be eaten by vultures.

Introducer: And sure enough, judgement did fall on the family of Ahab and Jezebel.

NEW TESTAMENT
James 4:1–10

CAST
Introducer: As above
James: No specific comments

Introducer: Jesus' brother James wrote some strong words about wrong desires.

James: What is causing the quarrels and fights among you? Isn't it the whole army of evil desires at war within you? You want what you don't have, so you scheme and kill to get it. You are jealous for what others have, and you can't possess it, so you fight and quarrel to take it away from them. And yet the reason you don't have what you want is that you don't ask God for it. And even when you do ask, you don't get it because your whole motive is wrong – you want only what will give you pleasure. You adulterers! Don't you realise that friendship with this world makes you an enemy of God? I say it again, that if your aim is to enjoy this world, you can't be a friend of God. What do you think the Scriptures mean when they say that the Holy Spirit, whom God has placed within us, jealously longs for us to be faithful? He gives us more and more strength to stand against such evil desires. As the Scriptures say, 'God sets himself against the proud, but he shows favour to the humble.'

So humble yourselves before God. Resist the Devil, and he will flee from you. Draw close to God, and God will draw close to you. Wash your hands, you sinners; purify your hearts, you hypocrites. Let there be tears for the wrong things you have done. Let there be sorrow and deep grief. Let there be sadness instead of laughter, and gloom instead of joy. When you bow down before the Lord and admit your dependence on him, he will lift you up and give you honour.

5) POEM BY STEWART HENDERSON

The poverty of palaces
the opulence of less –
this, my shepherd's wisdom.
I watch you crave redress
with lotteries as elixirs
for life's exacting toll –
all this yearning – temporal –
your heart, a begging bowl.

And you explain your passions
with a 'Que sera, sera',
through shiny assignations
in your cobwebbed Mardi Gras.
But Shangri-la is shuttered;
Nirvana's dank with mould.
True treasures are conundrums,
like shanty towns of gold.

The perfumes of Arabia
the linens of the East.
My bequests that should
dumbfound you,
I will lavish
on the least.

DO NOT COVET

Commandment 10: Exodus 20:17 'Do not covet your neighbour's house. Do not covet your neighbour's wife, male or female servant, ox or donkey, or anything else your neighbour owns.'

To covet means to desire to possess a thing; to want to take possession of something or someone that is not yours to have. In Moses' day the temptation was to take someone else's spouse, wealth (servants), their means of getting a livelihood (ox), their means of transport (donkey) or anything else they had. Nothing has really changed. We still look around and say to ourselves I wouldn't mind their wife or husband, I wouldn't mind their house, car, job, their computer and so on.

Now it is important to realise that the Bible is not against desire or ambition. Many desires are good things.

- In 1 Kings 8:58 Solomon prays 'May he (God) give us the desire to do his will in everything and to obey all the commands, laws, and regulations that he gave our ancestors'.
- Jesus himself urged 'us to hunger and thirst after righteousness'.
- Paul was ambitious to preach the gospel where it had never been preached. Even more ordinary desire is not wrong. There is nothing wrong with a husband desiring his wife or vice versa; there is nothing wrong with wanting a decent standard of living, a good job or desiring any of the good things that God has given us.

So what is wrong about coveting? The answer is that it is a wrong desire. It is a desire to want something that is not ours and which belongs to someone else.

WHAT'S WRONG WITH COVETING?

Let me outline four things that are wrong with coveting.

Coveting is idolatry

In Colossians 3:5 we read this 'So put to death the sinful, earthly things lurking within you. Have nothing to do with sexual sin, impurity, lust, and shameful desires. Don't be greedy for the good things of this life, for that is idolatry.'

How is coveting idolatry? Coveting is idolatry in three ways.

Firstly, by coveting we let things, not God, become the centre of our hearts. Coveting dethrones God and puts things in his place. But as Christians we are to find our fulfilment in knowing God; he alone is to be our joy and pleasure. The problem is that things take over that role. Possessions pretend to give us lasting peace and contentment. In fact they do neither; they become something that comes between us and God. Instead of turning to God for hope and encouragement, our emotions drift to things and possessions to seek fulfilment.

Secondly, by coveting we let things, not God, become the centre of our minds. The Bible teaches that we are to constantly think about God, to meditate on him and to daily consider all that he is and has done for us. But by coveting, our minds become full of things instead. We become obsessed by our objects of desire, whether they are cars or clothes. We read advertisements rather than God's word, we fill our time with shopping rather than by serving him. In coveting, God becomes shifted to the edge of our thought-life.

Thirdly, by coveting we let things, not God, become the centre of our wills. In worshipping things by coveting them, we let them govern our lives. The only rule of life for the covetous person is this: how can I get what I want? And things have no morality; they let us do what we want and how we want. Coveting rejects the lordship of God. You see, when we become Christians we admit that God is our heavenly father and that he knows what is best for us. That is why we pray to him for 'our daily bread'. By making him our Lord we accept that he is the wisest judge of what is good for us. 'My heavenly Father knows best' is a very Christian statement. We should be content to leave it to God whether we are to have riches or just enough. But coveting takes our lives away from under his rule. In coveting we say 'I know best!' Now of course by doing that, what we are saying to God is that he is not Lord, we are Lord. We are putting ourselves above him.

Coveting then is idolatry because it takes over the role of God in controlling what we desire, what we think and how we act. However there are other problems with coveting.

Coveting leads to other sins

One of the main problems with coveting is that, although it is a sin of the mind, it does not stay as a sin of the mind. Coveting almost always leads to other things. It has a subtle and creeping influence, and to the bad. In the story of Ahab and Naboth's vineyard the downward spiral started with a desire and then – with a little help from Jezebel – the affair slid first into lying, then into stealing and finally into murder.

Jesus himself makes plain the danger of what we think. In Mark 7:14–23 we read 'Then Jesus called to the crowd to come and hear. "All of you listen," he said, "and try to understand. You are not defiled by what you eat; you are defiled by what you say and do!" Then Jesus went into a house to get away from the crowds, and his disciples asked him what he meant by the statement he had made. "Don't you understand either?" he asked. "Can't you see that what you eat won't defile you? Food doesn't come in contact with your heart, but only passes through the stomach and then comes out again."' (By saying this, he showed that every kind of food is acceptable.) And then he added, '"It is the thought-life that defiles you. For from within, out of a person's heart, come evil thoughts, sexual immorality, theft, murder, adultery, greed, wickedness, deceit, eagerness for lustful pleasure, envy, slander, pride, and foolishness. All these vile things come from within; they are what defile you and make you unacceptable to God."'

It is very easy to say of coveting 'why is the Bible so concerned about what is simply something that goes on in our thoughts?' The answer that Jesus gives is that our thoughts are the things that defile us and lead us into sinful actions. Your thought-life matters!

Coveting stops us being generous

Coveting stops us from loving our neighbour. In its very nature, coveting puts self first. The covetous person is always looking at other people to see what they can get from them. With covetousness our lives become bottomless pits and we hunger after other people's wealth and possessions.

Now of course this is totally against everything that Jesus taught. In Acts 20:35 we read that Jesus said 'it is more blessed to give than to receive'. The pattern of living that Jesus sets out and that the rest of the New Testament describes is a life that looks to other people not to take, but to share and to give them what we have. Coveting turns us from being outward-looking into inward-looking; from being generous to being selfish. It is difficult to imagine how you can have a sharing and caring community of people where coveting is the rule of life. Covetousness corrodes a church.

Coveting cheats us of contentment

It is worth remembering that the commandments are given by God for our good. They are not hoops that God sadistically expects us to jump through. God is against coveting because it is bad for us.

Coveting robs us of contentment in this life. Everyone is agreed that coveting does not satisfy. Once you give in to it you can never have enough things. People decide that they will be happy if only they have this new hi-fi, that new computer, this new car, that new house and so on. This, they feel as they read the brochures or walk round the stores and showrooms, will guarantee them lasting and permanent satisfaction. Of course it doesn't. Never mind, they say vaguely disappointed, the next item on the list will satisfy. It never does. It is like walking to the horizon. The nearer you get the further away it retreats. Covetous people can never get enough to fulfil their wants.

In Matthew 6:19–21 Jesus advises us to lay up treasures in heaven. 'Don't store up treasures here on earth, where they can be eaten by moths and get rusty, and where thieves break in and steal. Store your treasures in heaven, where they will never become moth-eaten or rusty and where they will be safe from thieves. Wherever your treasure is, there your heart and thoughts will also be.'

Many of us are very wise about how we invest on earth, whether it is in houses, pension schemes or stocks and shares. But Jesus reminds us that the best and safest investment is in heaven. In some cases covetousness can completely stop people from becoming Christians by blinding them to their need for God. In this case their loss will be an appalling one; they will have traded an awesome future glory that can never perish for short-lived and unsatisfactory pleasures that they cannot keep hold of.

Yet the Bible also teaches that Christians will be assessed on how well they have been stewards of what God has given them in this life (I Corinthians 3:10–15; Luke 19:11–26). There is a real danger of us losing eternal reward by being distracted by earthly desires. Covetousness blinds us to our real duty here on earth; serving God and his kingdom.

SO HOW DO WE CHANGE?
Let me suggest three ways of how we keep our lives free of coveting.

We must be aware of the danger of coveting

The subtle sins are the most deadly. Coveting is everywhere. It's approved by society and it's easy to do. No one can tell when you covet; it's the invisible sin. You can even do it in church while pretending to listen to a sermon.

We need to realise that while there are good desires, there are also bad ones. We need also to realise that the society that we live in shapes our desires and wants to encourage us to covet. But the source of the problem is not advertising, or the media; it is our own hearts. The heart of the human problem is the problem of the human heart.

Perhaps I can suggest that during the next week we evaluate ourselves and try to answer the following questions.

- What are my main desires?
- Are they good or bad desires?
- To what extent do these desires control how I live, how I relate to others and how I spend my money?
- Do I believe that having these desires granted would give me contentment?
- What are my priorities?
- What should they be?

You may well find that you are driven to seek God in repentance at the awareness that how much covetousness there is in your life.

We must realign our desires

When a plane drifts off course the pilot will carefully change direction to get the aircraft back on its true course. We need to do something similar with our lives.

One of the problems with coveting is that we set our hearts on what is totally inadequate. After all, God wants us to set our hearts on him. As Saint Augustine said centuries ago, 'You have made our hearts, Lord, for yourself, and they are restless until they find their rest in you.' No amount of possessions, or pleasures can permanently satisfy the human heart. Only God can give us lasting satisfaction. We need to sit down and tell ourselves that all we have fixed our hearts on in this world is totally unsatisfying.

True contentment is only to be found in the right relationship with Christ. The reason for this is that this is how we were made. From the opening chapters of the Bible to the last it is clear that God desires us; our love and our friendship. God does not want robots or slaves; he wants children who love him. We were made for him and coveting things is a poor substitute for knowing God.

I suggest that you practice reminding yourself again and again that your true purpose is to know God through Christ and your only lasting joy is to be found there. Whenever the temptation to desire something that is not yours to have comes upon you, remind yourself that Jesus alone gives a real peace of mind.

It is also good for us to remind ourselves that the only safe thing for us to desire is the love of Jesus Christ. Everything else that we set our hearts on will cheat or fail us. Indeed to those who come to him Jesus makes a wonderful promise. 'So do not worry, saying, "What shall we eat?" or "What shall we drink?" or "What shall we wear?" For the pagans run after all these things, and your heavenly Father knows that you need them. But seek first his kingdom and his righteousness, and all these things will be given to you as well' (Matthew 6:31–33 NIV). If you serve Jesus you can have your cake and eat it. If you do not serve Jesus you will find that you neither have the cake nor eat it.

We need to focus our hearts on Jesus and not on our desires.

We must keep our hearts in shape

But it is not enough to do this only once. You do not stay fit by running one race; you need to keep your fitness by exercise. This is true here. Let me give you some tips.

First, have contempt for covetousness. Keep reminding yourself how futile it is to set your heart on anything else other than Jesus. Resist the temptation to believe that 'just one more thing' can bring you happiness. Learn to see through the claims and promises of advertisements.

Secondly, acquire an attitude of gratitude. Learn to thank God for what he has given you. The Apostle Paul said, 'I have learnt to be content whatever the circumstances' (Philippians

4:11). He was in prison when he said this, but he was able to rejoice in his difficult circumstances. It is sometimes trite and simplistic to say 'count your blessings'. Nevertheless the idea of listing in what ways we have been blessed is one that is very valuable. Now doing this may be an act of the will; it may be something that we have to force ourselves to do. But as we do it is very likely that our hearts will follow. We need to practice being grateful.

Thirdly, be a wise steward. God has graciously given a vast amount to all of us. We need to take what he has given us and use it wisely. It is often a temptation to look out for more when we are unable to look after what we have already. Linked with this should come the healthy realisation that the more we have we been given the greater that we are responsible for.

Fourthly, focus on relationships, not things. 'Better to be poor and reverence the LORD than to be rich and in trouble. Better to eat vegetables with people you love than to eat the finest meat where there is hate' (Proverbs 15:16–17 GNB).

In the race for riches and possessions people can be sacrificed. People however are eternal and things are merely temporary. Relationships have a lasting value. God desires for us to have good relationship not only with him but also with each other. The call is to love people and use things; so often the world has this wisdom the other way about; to love things and use people. Ask yourself, how are your relationships? If someone looked at your lifestyle, at your time, at your bank statement, what would they show about the value you put on relationships?

Finally, be a giver. The best antidote to coveting is a brutal one: it is to be freely generous with what we have already. The best remedy for covetousness is to be someone who gives away generously, whether money or possessions. Jesus talked a great deal about giving. The weed of covetousness finds it hard to become rooted in the soil of a generous heart.

We all have a choice. We can covet – and we will find we have cheated ourselves.

We can let Christ live in us and clean us – and we can be contented; both in this life and in the life to come.

7) SUGGESTED PRAYERS

A COVENANT WITH GOD

The following prayer comes from the Methodist church covenant service [C D.2].

[Leader]: Lord God, Holy Father, since you have called us through Christ to share in this gracious Covenant, we take upon ourselves with joy the yoke of obedience, and, for love of you, engage ourselves to seek and do your perfect will. We are no longer our own but yours.

[All together]: I am no longer my own but yours. Put me to what you will, rank me with whom you will; put me to doing, put me to suffering; let me be employed for you or laid aside for you, exalted for you or brought low for you; let me be full, let me be empty; let me have all things, let me have nothing; I freely and wholeheartedly yield all things to your pleasure and disposal. And now, glorious and blessed God, Father, Son and Holy Spirit, you are mine and I am yours. So be it. And the covenant now made on earth, let it be ratified in heaven. Amen.

PRAYER OF CONFESSION

We acknowledge O Lord that much of what our heart's desire is neither good nor right. Our hearts are deceitful above all things and beyond cure and only you can understand them.

We come before you now, and in a moment of silence, confess to you those things that we have wrongly desired.

[Silence]

We thank you for the many promises of forgiveness that are held out in Scripture to those who are truly repentant. Let us take to ourselves God's promise in Ezekiel 36. 'I will sprinkle clean water on you and you will be clean; I will cleanse you from all impurities and from all idols. I will give you a new heart and put a new spirit in new; I will remove from you your heart of stone and give you a heart of flesh. And I will put my spirit in you and move you to follow my decrees and be careful to obey my laws' (Ezekiel 36:25–27).

We pray O Lord that you will, indeed cleanse us from our wrong desires and infill us with your Holy Spirit, through Jesus Christ our Lord, Amen.

PRAYER OF COMMITMENT

O Lord, our God you know the depths of our hearts and the shallowness of our desires. Open our eyes to the deceitfulness of the things of this world and the eternal value of knowing you and doing your will.

We ask that, through your Spirit, we are enabled to love you and to make you the true focus of our lives. We praise you and glorify you because of your greatness. We acknowledge that in you – and in you alone – we find the true desires of our hearts.

Help us Lord to be able to think more of you and to know you so well that the temptations to covet the things of this world will have little attraction. Grant us O Lord, right desires and help us to hunger and thirst for righteousness and the coming of your kingdom. Keep us single-hearted in our love for you.

We ask these things through Jesus Christ our Lord, Amen.

Don't Lie!

Commandment 9: Exodus 20: 16 'Do not testify falsely against your neighbour.'

1) SUGGESTED HYMNS & SONGS
HYMNS
- O, for a thousand tongues to sing
- Great is thy faithfulness
- O that the Lord would guide my ways [Isaac Watts]
- All people that on earth do dwell (there is a good modern *Jubilate Hymns* version)
- God the Lord, the king Almighty [Christopher Idle, *Jubilate Hymns*]

SONGS
- Many are the words we speak (Now to live the life)
- Faithful One
- You are God in heaven
- Justice and mercy [Matt Redman]
- Who can sound the depths of sorrow in the Father heart of God
- We'll walk the land with hearts on fire

2) WARM-UP ACTIVITIES & ILLUSTRATIONS
Either

ANECDOTE

Point out that when human beings use words their meaning can change very rapidly. The following sequences of memos regarding Halley's Comet are alleged to have appeared in an American school.

(i) MEMO to Assistant Superintendent from Superintendent:
Next Thursday at 10:30 a.m. Halley's Comet will appear over this area. This is an event which occurs only once every 75 years. Call the principals and have them assemble their teachers and classes on the athletic fields and explain this phenomenon to them. If it rains, then cancel the day's observation and have the classes meet in the auditorium to see a film about the Comet.

(ii) MEMO to Principals from Assistant Superintendent:
By order of the Superintendent of Schools next Thursday at 10:30 a.m. Halley's Comet will appear over your athletic field. If it rains, then cancel the day's classes and report to the auditorium with your teachers and students where you will show films – a phenomenal event which occurs every 75 years.

(iii) MEMO to Teachers from Principal:
By order of the phenomenal Superintendent of Schools, at 10:30 a.m. next Thursday Halley's Comet will appear in the auditorium. In case of rain over the athletic fields the superintendent will give another order – something which occurs only every 75 years.

(iv) MEMO to Students from Teachers:
Next Thursday at 10:30 a.m. the Superintendent of Schools will appear in our school auditorium with Halley's Comet – something which occurs every 75 years. If it rains the Superintendent

will cancel the comet and order us all out to our phenomenal athletic field.

(v) MEMO to Parents from Students:
When it rains next Thursday at 10:30 a.m. over the school athletic field, the phenomenal 75-year-old Superintendent of Schools will cancel all classes and appear before the whole school in the auditorium, accompanied by Bill Halley and the Comets.

[Note: Occurring in various forms on the Internet; origin unknown.]

Or

PARTICIPATORY QUESTIONS
Explain that you want to carry out a survey.

(i) Give the definition of TOTAL HONESTY

- You tell no lies
- Make no deceptions
- Never gossip
- Make no exaggerations or misleading statements

Now ask for people to raise their hands if their life over the past week has scored a hundred percent on the TOTAL HONESTY scale.
> What about 95%?
> What about 90%? etc.

[Note: Stop fairly soon to avoid embarrassment to the honest! To ease any awkwardness you might want to make a joke about whether we can be trusted to be honest about our honesty.]

(ii) Again ask for a show of hands. Consider the following:

- How many of you would go to a doctor you knew was a liar?
- How many of you would accept financial advice from someone who was a liar?
- How many of you would get your car repaired by someone you knew was a liar?
- How many of you would give money to a charity run by someone who was a liar?
- How many of you would consider marrying someone who was a liar?
- How many of you would buy a history book written by someone you knew was a liar?

[Note: From these questions you should probably be able to conclude two things. First, we admit that we personally are far from being totally honest. Secondly, we hate lies and distrust people who make them.]

3) CHILDREN'S ACTIVITY
PREPARATION
- Four tubes of cheap toothpaste
- A table with a plastic cloth
- Four coloured plates

ACTIVITY
Ask for four volunteers to come to the front and give each one of them a tube of toothpaste. The first part of this competition is for them to make the most creative design on the plates using all the toothpaste in the tube. Give them 90 seconds to do this. After this time get other people to judge which is best.

Now reveal the second part of the competition. This is for the contestants to get as much toothpaste back into the tube as they can. After a couple of seconds trying they will give up.

[Note: They will be covered in toothpaste so you will need to have a place that they can go and wash.]

CONCLUSION

Before the children leave to get cleaned up make the point that toothpaste can't be put back in its tube. The Bible says that in the same way neither can we put our words back in our mouth once we have spoken them. So it is important to think about the words we say.

4) BIBLE READINGS

OLD TESTAMENT

I suggest two linked passages from Genesis, both of which lend themselves to being read dramatically.

Genesis 2:15-16; 3:1-24

CAST
Introducer: As in Service One
Text Narrator: As in Service One
Serpent: An attractive smooth voice
The LORD: As in Service One
Eve: Innocent at first and then guilty and defensive
Adam: Similarly guilty and defensive

Introducer: In the first pages of the Bible we read how, a long time ago, God created the first man and woman and placed them in a fertile garden where they had everything they could want. In giving them everything God made only one restriction.

Text Narrator: The LORD God placed the man in the Garden of Eden to tend and care for it. But the LORD God gave him this warning:

The LORD: You may freely eat any fruit in the garden except fruit from the tree of the knowledge of good and evil. If you eat of its fruit, you will surely die.

Introducer: The Bible tells how God made a woman, Eve, to be a companion for Adam. Then, sometime later a strange visitor appeared in the garden.

Text Narrator: Now the serpent was the shrewdest of all the creatures the LORD God had made...

Serpent: Did God really say you must not eat any of the fruit in the garden?

Eve: Of course we may eat it. It's only the fruit from the tree at the centre of the garden that we are not allowed to eat. God says we must not eat it or even touch it, or we will die.

Serpent: You won't die! God knows that your eyes will be opened when you eat it. You will become just like God, knowing everything, both good and evil.

Text Narrator: The woman was convinced. The fruit looked so fresh and delicious, and it would make her so wise! So she ate some of the fruit. She also gave some to her husband, who was with her. Then he ate it, too. At that moment, their eyes were opened, and they suddenly felt shame at their nakedness. So they strung fig leaves together around their hips to cover themselves. Toward evening they heard the LORD God walking about in the garden, so they hid themselves among the trees. The LORD God called to Adam.

The LORD: Where are you?

Adam: I heard you, so I hid. I was afraid because I was naked.

The LORD: Who told you that you were naked? Have you eaten the fruit I commanded you not to eat?

Adam: Yes, but it was the woman you gave me who brought me the fruit, and I ate it.

Text Narrator: Then the LORD God asked the woman...

The LORD: How could you do such a thing?

Eve: The serpent tricked me. That's why I ate it.

Text Narrator: So the LORD God said to the serpent...

The LORD: Because you have done this, you will be punished. You are singled out from all the domestic and wild animals of the whole earth to be cursed. You will grovel in the dust as long as you live, crawling along on your belly. From now on, you and the woman will be enemies, and your offspring and her offspring will be enemies. He will crush your head, and you will strike his heel.

Text Narrator: Then the LORD God said to the woman...

The LORD: You will bear children with intense pain and suffering. And though your desire will be for your husband, he will be your master.

Text Narrator: Then the LORD God said to Adam...

The LORD: Because you listened to your wife and ate the fruit I told you not to eat, I have placed a curse on the ground. All your life you will struggle to scratch a living from it. It will grow thorns and thistles for you, though you will eat of its grains. All your life you will sweat to produce food, until your dying day. Then you will return to the ground from which you came. For you were made from dust, and to the dust you will return.

Text Narrator: Then Adam named his wife Eve, because she would be the mother of all people everywhere. And the LORD God made clothing from animal skins for Adam and his wife. Then the LORD God said...

The LORD: The people have become as we are, knowing everything, both good and evil. What if they eat the fruit of the tree of life? Then they will live forever!

Text Narrator: So the LORD God banished Adam and his wife from the Garden of Eden, and he sent Adam out to cultivate the ground from which he had been made. After banishing them from the garden, the LORD God stationed mighty angelic beings to the east of Eden. And a flaming sword flashed back and forth, guarding the way to the tree of life.

NEW TESTAMENT
John 8:31–59

CAST
Introducer: As in Service One
Text Narrator: As in Service One
Jesus: Ideally, the voice of Jesus should be tough but loving, warm but sorrowful, ordinary but extraordinary, gentle but with a hard edge of judgement underneath and authoritative without any hint of arrogance. Other than that – it's easy! Specifically, here he should speak strongly. It would also be helpful for there to be a slight emphasis on the formula 'I tell you the truth'. On his final answer '…before Abraham was born, I am,' there should be a sharp ringing emphasis on the 'I am'. (It is a phrase used by God of himself in the Old Testament.)
Crowd: Should be a number of people of both sexes. Increasingly angry. The 'We are not illegitimate children' is presumably a dig at Jesus; snide allegations about his birth were probably already widespread.

Introducer: In Chapter Eight of John's gospel we read in verses 31–59 how Jesus came under opposition in Jerusalem. As he talked with the increasingly hostile crowd the whole question of the truth came up.

Text Narrator: Jesus said to the people who believed in him…

Jesus: You are truly my disciples if you keep obeying my teachings. And you will know the truth, and the truth will set you free.

Crowd: But we are descendants of Abraham. We have never been slaves to anyone on earth. What do you mean, 'set free'?

Jesus: I assure you that everyone who sins is a slave of sin. A slave is not a permanent member of the family, but a son is part of the family forever. So if the Son sets you free, you will indeed be free. Yes, I realize that you are descendants of Abraham. And yet some of you are trying to kill me because my message does not find a place in your hearts. I am telling you what I saw when I was with my Father. But you are following the advice of your father.

Crowd: Our father is Abraham.

Jesus: No, for if you were children of Abraham, you would follow his good example. I told you the truth I heard from God, but you are trying to kill me. Abraham wouldn't do a thing like that. No, you are obeying your real father when you act that way.

Crowd: We are not illegitimate children! Our true Father is God himself.

Jesus: If God were your Father, you would love me, because I have come to you from God. I am not here on my own, but he sent me. Why can't you understand what I am saying? It is because you are unable to do so! For you are the children of your father the Devil, and you love to do the evil things he does. He was a murderer from the beginning and has always hated the truth. There is no truth in him. When he lies, it is consistent with his character; for he is a liar and the father of lies. So when I tell the truth, you just naturally don't believe me! Which of you can truthfully accuse me of sin? And since I am telling you the truth, why don't you believe me? Anyone whose Father is God listens gladly to the words of God. Since you don't, it proves you aren't God's children.

Crowd: You Samaritan devil! Didn't we say all along that you were possessed by a demon?

Jesus: No. I have no demon in me. For I honour my Father – and you dishonour me. And though I have no wish to glorify myself, God wants to glorify me. Let him be the judge. I assure you, anyone who obeys my teaching will never die!

Crowd: Now we know you are possessed by a demon. Even Abraham and the prophets died, but you say that those who obey your teaching will never die! Are you greater than our father Abraham, who died? Are you greater than the prophets, who died? Who do you think you are?

Jesus: If I am merely boasting about myself, it doesn't count. But it is my Father who says these glorious things about me. You say, 'He is our God', but you do not even know him. I know him. If I said otherwise, I would be as great a liar as you! But it is true – I know him and obey him. Your ancestor Abraham rejoiced as he looked forward to my coming. He saw it and was glad.

Crowd: You aren't even fifty years old. How can you say you have seen Abraham?

Jesus: The truth is before Abraham was, *I am*.

Text Narrator: At that point they picked up stones to kill him. But Jesus hid himself from them and left the Temple.

5) POEM BY STEWART HENDERSON

The dictionary of Satan,
the scraping of his hoof.
On the horns of a dilemma,
the goring of the Truth.

Don't think of it as falsehood
more like getting by.
In order to be honest
it's requisite to lie.

For candidness is messy
and honesty's naive,
sincerity will cost you
it's fitting to deceive.

Before your resignation,
your praises will be sung,
I'm not so much spin doctor –
more plastic surgeon of the tongue.

And treason has its martyrs
and perjury its saints,
I've renamed these commandments
ten miserly complaints.

The dictionary of Satan,
the scraping of his hoof.
On the horns of a dilemma,
the goring of the Truth.

6) SERMON

DO NOT LIE

Commandment 9: Exodus 20:16 'Do not testify falsely against your neighbour.'

[Note: Because of the fact that there are many complex issues to do with truth and lies I have given here two outlines; one is a short talk/sermon while the other is one of more substantial length. In fact they cover slightly different ground.]

SHORT SERMON: WATCHING OUR WORDS

After all we have said and thought so far today the power of the tongue should be clear. Yet we do not realise it; the fact is that we live in a society of truth decay. And it's rotting not just our mouths but our personal lives and relationships.

Why do we tell lies? One of the reasons is that we don't want to take responsibility for the things that we do. The disease of BSE is widespread – Blame Someone Else. It began in the Garden of Eden and has affected and infected every descendant of Adam and Eve since.

It shows really the state of our hearts. As Jesus' brother James said, 'People can tame all kinds of animals and birds and reptiles and fish, but no one can tame the tongue. It is an uncontrollable evil, full of deadly poison. Sometimes it praises our Lord and Father, and sometimes it breaks out into curses against those who have been made in the image of God. And so blessing and cursing come pouring out of the same mouth. Surely, my brothers and sisters, this is not right! Does a spring of water bubble out with both fresh water and bitter water? Can you pick olives from a fig tree or figs from a grapevine? No, and you can't draw fresh water from a salty pool' (James 3:7–12).

Whilst we are confronted time and time again with the widespread extent of lies within the world, whether in presidents, politicians, the tabloid newspapers or our own lives, the way God conducts himself is in stark contrast.

God is the one who is always true. He never lies or is unfaithful. Whereas we often say, 'I don't know why he or she did that; it is so out of character', God never does anything which we could say is out of character. He not only speaks truth, he *is* truth. So consider Jesus. A man who practised what he preached, who lived truthfully and spoke of a faithful, trustworthy God who proved himself to be true in his own life by raising him from the dead.

God is not only the one who is truly true, everything that we do, say, think and hear happens before him. Nothing is hidden from his sight. He cannot be hidden from, shut out, or consigned to a side alley. Whether we like it or not, nothing is hidden from him.

On the cross Jesus paid the price for our lies and untruth. He took responsibility for the sins that we refuse to take responsibility for. And because of his death, resurrection and the gift of the Holy Spirit we can be offered a new start; forgiveness, transformation and the power to live a different life.

It is quite clear that, for the Christian, a new and different standard of truth is expected. Listen to what Paul says in Ephesians: 'Don't use foul or abusive language. Let everything you say be good and helpful, so that your words will be an encouragement to those who hear them… Get rid of all bitterness, rage, anger, harsh words, and slander, as well as all types of malicious behaviour' (Ephesians 4:29,31). And in Colossians, Paul writes this: 'But now is the time to get rid of anger, rage, malicious behaviour, slander, and dirty language. Don't lie to each other, for you have stripped off your old evil nature and all its wicked deeds' (Colossians 3:8-9).

We are called to be truthful in our speech, to be aware of just how powerful or words are and to try and tame the tongue.

Speaking the truth

Avoid lies: We all need to be on our guard the whole time of the human trait we all have to cover up and not to take responsibility. We need to be people and communities of honesty; this will mean a readiness for forgiveness. If we are living a life of deceit – living a lie – then we should talk to somebody we can trust about that immediately. We must seek to live in the light not the darkness.

Avoid gossip: Part of bearing false witness is gossiping. The Book of Proverbs talks about gossip being like delicious food, like choice morsels. Huge amounts of money and livelihoods are made on spreading gossip; think of all the magazines and newspapers that are based on it. We as the truthful people of God are to be different. We should never take joy or delight in anyone else's misfortune (see 1 Corinthians 13), nor should we spread rumours behind people's backs. When tempted to pass on gossip we should ask ourselves, 'Am I prepared to put my name to this?' If we are concerned about something we hear, we should go directly to the person concerned. Don't be a muck-spreader. Be unwilling to either give or to receive gossip.

Be encouragers: The Bible urges us to speak the truth in love. As a modern-day proverb says, 'Lord may my words be sweet and tender, for tomorrow I may have to eat them'.

Be true to your word: Jesus encourages us to let our 'yes' be 'yes' and our 'no' be 'no'. We are to be people who say what we mean and mean what we say. We must be careful therefore before promising things and before committing ourselves. Whatever else those around us say about our Christian lives let them not be able to say that we are hypocrites.

Be a listener: God gave us all two ears and only one mouth. Let us learn to use them in correspondence with that fact. Let us think before we speak and take time to listen to others.

Be accountable: We must have relationships where we have a commitment to openness and honesty. We need to find people who we can share weaknesses with and who will ask us the difficult questions and whom we have promised to tell the truth.

Before God let us pledge ourselves to faithfulness in all the different ways that we speak.

LONG SERMON: LIES OR TRUTH?
[Note: This could easily be divided into two parts (Lies and Truth). These could be separated by a hymn.]

INTRODUCTION
As we saw just now, we have a curious double standard to lying. We expect to be lied to, we expect we will have to lie ourselves, yet it is something that we dislike and despise. We know that it is wrong.

The setting of this commandment is plain; it is the law court. What is prohibited is testifying against someone falsely; for example, saying that you saw someone commit a crime when you didn't. Of course, in a society where there was capital punishment, telling lies in court could easily be fatal. Honest witnesses are key things in any society; it is no accident that outside the church the only public place in Britain where the Bible is still used is when people make oaths upon it in legal courts. In fact so seriously was the crime of lying in a court situation taken in Old Testament times that false witnesses were dealt with very severely. In Deuteronomy 19:16–19 we read the following 'If a malicious witness comes forward and accuses someone of a crime, then both the accuser and accused must appear before the priests and judges who are on duty before the LORD. They must be closely questioned, and if the accuser is found to be lying, the accuser will receive the punishment intended for the accused. In this way, you will cleanse such evil from among you.' In other words if you were a false witness in a case that had the death penalty attached to it then, by a stern if fair logic, you would be sentenced to death.

Yet this commandment has always been taken to go well beyond the law court. It rules that, as God's people, we are not to lie in any form and that we are to uphold the truth.

Yet the whole issue of truth and lies needs some careful thought. When we think of liars we may think of people who have been involved in spectacular cases of fraud or political scandal and whose names have been front page in our newspapers. We can think of cases in history; for example Joseph Stalin who said, 'Of all the treasures a State can possess, the human lives of its citizens are for us the most precious.' Not bad for man who is held to be responsible for over 30 million deaths. There are many instances we can think of in law cases where people have pleaded innocence, only to be proved guilty. *[Note: You might give some local and topical examples.]* As with the other commandments we think that this one really only applies to people much worse than us.

Yet there is far more to bearing false witness than this.

TYPES OF FALSE WITNESS

When we look at the whole idea of bearing false witness we find that there are many different ways for us to abuse the truth. Let me list some:

The outright lie

The most obvious type of untruth is the complete lie where there is a total fabrication of new facts.

The most spectacular examples of this sort of thing are of course those lies that make the papers or the law courts. Tax fraud, bigamy, getting a job by giving dishonest information, obtaining money by false pretences, making misleading advertisements. But these big lies are only the tip of the iceberg. For every one lie like this there are a million baby ones where ordinary people like you or I tell complete falsehoods. How often do people say, 'Do you know I was just going to phone you!', 'Oh I did ring but your line was engaged', 'Our other department must have your file', 'Ah yes we have had a computer problem' or that old stand-by – 'The dog ate it'. Dogs – and computers – are very useful because they can never give their side of the story.

Now in the story of the Garden of Eden we have this sort of outright lie from the serpent who, the Bible later tells us, is Satan, the devil. Here the serpent says to the woman (Genesis 3:4–5), 'You won't die! God knows that your eyes will be opened when you eat it. You will become just like God, knowing everything, both good and evil.'

This is a total and shameless denial of God's warning about the consequences of eating the forbidden fruit. With it is an equally false promise of what would happen when Adam and Eve ate the fruit.

It is hardly surprising in the light of this, that in John's gospel (John 8:44), we read Jesus' comment to the hostile crowd: 'For you are the children of your father the Devil, and you love to do the evil things he does. He was a murderer from the beginning and has always hated the truth. There is no truth in him. When he lies, it is consistent with his character; for he is a liar and the father of lies.'

Jesus here makes the point that Satan not only speaks lies but spreads lies. For us to use lies is to follow the devil. We must be very watchful that we do not make any sort of outright lie.

But the outright lie is not the only form of untruth that there is. There are far more subtle forms.

The insinuation

One common form of dishonesty is the insinuation. An insinuation is where you make a statement that leads people to think something that is not true. It is not quite an outright lie; instead we just encourage them to jump to conclusions. We provide the building blocks and let them construct the lie themselves. The attraction of the insinuation is that it be done so subtly that no one notices it has been done. And of course because we haven't actually told a lie we are able to walk away with a clear conscience. Making insinuations is lying by stealth.

Let me give you an example. Imagine that Anne has got a new job. 'Ah,' says Billy quietly, 'I hope she sticks this one out.' Immediately you start to wonder whether Anne has a problem in perseverance. And before long you have begun to imagine that Anne is an unstable person.

It is amazing what harm we can do by insinuation. Imagine that tomorrow evening someone asks you how your boss was at work and you reply with the single word 'Sober'. Now, of course they probably were sober, but by highlighting the fact you have managed to imply that there have been times when they were not. Do it a few times and very soon an entire history of alcohol abuse will have been invented. Insinuations can be enhanced by a gesture or a tone of voice. There are ways of taking a perfectly neutral statement such as 'Joan's gone to see the bank manager' and so pitching it that the hearer can assume that Joan is either bankrupt or engaged in adultery. [Do this.] And of course poor Joan has no come-back because you can say in your own defence 'I only said you'd gone to the bank manager'.

Not all insinuations are negative. In order to boost ourselves we can sometimes let slip little misleading pieces of information. 'Oh,' you might hear someone say, 'I once asked that question of X' where X is a hero figure among the group of people to whom they are talking. Now in reality it was in a question-and-answer session at a meeting of five hundred people twenty years ago but by careful emphasis the speaker can give the impression that they and X were the greatest of pals.

Insinuation is very common today. In fact it is one of the chief tools used by the 'spin doctors' who are now such a feature of British politics. Yet it has a long history. In fact if the outright lie goes back to the Devil in the Garden of Eden so does the insinuation. 'Did God really say "you must not eat any of the fruit in the garden?" the Serpent asked. "Really? Are you sure?"' You can feel how he is undermining Eve's belief and trust in God. But then as he gives the outright lie about dying there is yet more insinuation. '"You won't die! God knows that your eyes will be opened when you eat it. You will become just like God, knowing everything, both good and evil."'

The insinuation the Devil is making here is plain; 'God is preventing you from having something that is good for you for his own selfish reasons. God is a spoilsport.'

We need to watch out for insinuation both in our conversation and in that of others. It can easily be stopped if you challenge someone over what they have said. 'Why, that sounds like you are suggesting that... Did you mean to imply that?' You may be helped in resisting the temptation of the insinuation by remembering that the word 'insinuation' can be seen as a shortened form of an 'in-sin situation'.

The half-truth

Another clever way to achieve the effect of an outright lie but with less risk and effort is simply not to give the full picture. The phrase used in the legal courts is that we are 'to tell the truth the whole, truth and nothing but the truth' and only telling part of the truth is one way of bearing false witness. For example, someone may say to you that Mike had a blazing row with his wife. It may be true but it may easily overlook the fact that later both of them apologised to each other and have put it behind them. Half-truths have the advantage that they only require half the effort of an outright lie. In fact by telling a half-truth we may feel that we have not told a lie at all.

In the 'Spycatcher' trial of the 1980s, the Head of the Civil Service, Sir Robert Armstrong, made a much quoted comment about a letter. 'It contains a misleading impression, not a lie,' he said. 'It was being economical with the truth.' Sir Robert Armstrong was wrong; half a truth can be a lie.

At the start of human history, the Devil – the father of lies – was similarly economical with the truth. We read that he asked Eve 'Did God really say you must not eat any of the fruit in the garden?' In fact what God had said was this: 'You may freely eat any fruit in the garden except fruit from the tree of the knowledge of good and evil. If you eat of its fruit, you will surely die.' By twisting what God had actually said, Satan totally misrepresents God.

We need to beware of half-truths and to remember that they too are also lies. It is a shameful thing to tell only the part of a story that incriminates someone. We need to be sure when we tell or hear a story that we have the whole truth. When unsure, it is far better to give people the benefit of the doubt and ignore such tales.

The excuse

The excuse is a form of false witness that is all too common. By making an excuse we divert blame and shame from ourselves onto someone or something else. 'It's not my fault,' says the little child, 'It was Ben that did it.' Thirty years later the adult still says 'It's not my fault' only now he blames his upbringing, his neighbourhood or his genes.

Classic examples of excuses can be found in the account of Adam and Eve's temptation and act of disobedience. Notice what Adam says when God asks him whether he has eaten the fruit: 'Yes, but it was the woman you gave me who brought me the fruit, and I ate it.' Instead of taking responsibility he tries to pass the blame away from himself onto the woman (and by implication, God). When questioned, Eve in turn blames the serpent. '"The serpent tricked me," she replied. "That's why I ate it."'

Jesus called the Devil 'the father of lies'; and we see how true it is. Already Adam and Eve are following in his footsteps, obscuring the truth and trying to divert the blame away from themselves. 'It was someone else's fault' is the oldest of all human lies.

Yet making excuses can be doubly harmful. On the one hand it harms someone else; the blame has to land somewhere. On the other it can stop us from dealing with the problem. By transferring our guilt we have no opportunity to repent or deal with our problems; we simply go into denial mode. The Bible makes it plain that the only real solution to sin is to face up to it, admit it, repent of it and seek forgiveness from God.

Other ways of abusing truth

In addition to lies, insinuations, half-truths and excuses there are other forms of abusing the truth. One that is roundly condemned in the Bible is gossiping. I suppose this could be defined as sharing tales about someone without concern for either truth or love. It passes easily into slander. Gossip is enormously hurtful and churches are very vulnerable to it.

The story is told of three church ministers who go away on a long fishing trip together. In the course of this they become very confiding and one evening, one of them tearfully confesses his failings with pride and anger and urges the others to confess their sins and weaknesses. Convicted of the need to confess, the second minister then reveals how he has struggled for years with lust. They then look at the third man who for a long time stays silent. Finally, he speaks. 'My brothers, if you really want to know, my weakness is that I love to gossip. And I can hardly wait to get home and tell everybody!'

Where gossip reigns, who is prepared to be open and admit their failings and ask for help? How can there be trust and faith in this sort of situation? Gossip is a sort of social woodworm in the church; it slowly and quietly undermines all that we do.

Remember it takes two to gossip; one to give it and one to receive it. Refuse to listen to gossip and if someone seeks gossip from you either give them 'good gossip' by being positive or stay silent.

Flattery too is a form of lying although most of us think of it as being harmless. It has been described as the opposite of slander and it shares some of the same characteristics. Both the flatterer and the slanderer do not care for truth. It should be avoided because it devalues everything else we say.

Another problem area is exaggeration. Our modern world demands results and it is all too easy to be elastic with facts, especially when it makes us look good. Even churches are not immune from this; statistics on church membership or attendance figures are often 'generously' assessed.

Finally as far as lying goes, quite the easiest way of all is to lie by keeping silent. Imagine you are at a meeting where something untrue or hurtful is said about someone you know. What do you do? The temptation is to say nothing. The right thing is to stand up for the absent party, whatever it costs you.

WHY DO WE LIE?

Why do we find the truth so threatening that, so often, we try and avoid it?

Sometimes people lie because it's convenient. You know the sort of thing; 'If anyone rings, tell them I'm out'. It may be that we are lazy or we just don't want to face something or someone. There was once a music critic who, when asked by performers for a comment on some really terrible performance, would say 'memorable, truly memorable'. It's the easy way out. You can get this sort of thing at the end of a service. 'Thank you pastor/minister. Your sermon made me think.' (Think about what?) Or 'It was well up to your usual standard.' (Is that good or bad?)

Sometimes we lie to shift the blame and avoid punishment. 'It wasn't me, Dad!' or 'Honest boss, I don't know who missed those figures. I was working on something else.' Sometimes we lie to save ourselves embarrassment. 'Oh yes, Mrs Smith, of course I remember you.' 'Yes, I suppose we are lost; they must have changed the road signs.' We don't like to admit we are not perfect parents, spouses, teachers or preachers.

Sometimes we lie to boost our own self-image. We can do this by raising ourselves so, for example, we might say, 'Oh, I've advised some of the best people in the business on this sort of thing,' or 'I could do that with eyes closed'. Sometimes we aim for the same effect by lowering others; 'Them? Oh it's not really their area of expertise.' Or 'Oh, they try hard, but...' Many of us are so insecure that we think that the lie is an acceptable way of self-promotion.

The ultimate reason is quite simply that we put ourselves – and our own interests – above anything else, including truth. In a lot of non-Christian cultures truth is less important than saving face or making a good impression and the basis for answering a question is not 'what is the right answer?' but 'what answer do they want to hear?' Actually as western society slides away from its Christian framework, this is becoming common here. We need to take a stand and be known as people of truth.

HOW TO HOLD TO TRUTH
Let me briefly outline some ways of helping us hold onto truth.

We must realise that truth is vital

We need to remind ourselves that truth is essential for life. Once we switch to a way of living and speaking where truth is negotiable or even disposable then we are in enormous danger. Our lives have started sinking into a bog that has no footholds at all. The effects can be catastrophic.

In the first place, truth is vital for any sort of community to exist. The Biblical vision of the local church is of an open community of people who care for each other and who share their lives at the deepest of levels. Once lying gets a foothold here this goal becomes unworkable; lies, excuses and gossip soon eat away at the community and it disintegrates. In Acts 4 we read the chilling story of how, in the very early days of the church, Ananias and Sapphira lied about their giving, only to be struck dead as a result. Many people have found the story unacceptable to them; surely, they argue, God wouldn't do something like this? Yet once we realise how vital truth is to a community, we can see that if it had been left unchallenged the action of Ananias and Sapphira could have destroyed the embryonic church far more effectively than any persecution.

If lies are lethal for Christian communities they are also lethal for us as individuals. The picture that is given in the Bible of the human race is that we are sick and are in need of healing by God. But it is all too easy to lie and say about ourselves that 'there is no problem'. And if you deny that you are ill, it is hard to be healed. You see this very clearly in the story of the Pharisee and the tax collector in Luke 18:9–14. The Pharisee stands up and prays in the confidence that he is righteous and, as a result, God rejects him; the dishonest tax collector acknowledges the truth that he is a sinner, seeks mercy and, as a result, is forgiven by God.

The first step to any form of healing is to admit that we need treatment. The first essential step in our salvation is the recognition of the truth that we need God's forgiveness. Lying, in whatever form, denies the need for healing.

We need to be truthful people for the sake of the church community and also for the sake of ourselves.

We must realise that lying is serious

Part of the problem here is that because lying deals with words rather than things, we imagine that lies are not significant. After all, we say, they are only words, not actions. 'Sticks and stones will break my bones, but calling names won't hurt me', goes the saying, but broken bones can heal while the wounds caused by words may take years to mend. In many cases they never heal. We need to realise that our words do have weight; they can ruin lives and destroy relationships. Given how serious words are, we would be better thinking a lot more before we say them.

I have found the word THINK a helpful guide before saying something

> T – is it true?
> H – will it help?
> I – is it inspiring?
> N – is it necessary?
> K – is it kind?

If we can't answer yes to all of these then we shouldn't say it!

We must realise that Jesus is the truth

Jesus made it plain that there is a battle over truth and this is very plain in the passage in John 8:32–59 that we read as our second text.

- Three times here, Jesus uses the phrase 'I tell you the truth' or 'truly, truly'. This was his way of emphasising that his words were totally true.
- Jesus claims (8:32) that if someone follows him then they will know the truth, and the truth will set them free.
- Jesus declares to the crowd (8:40) that he tells them the truth from God.
- Jesus tells the crowd in (8:44) that the reason for their rejection of him is that they are children of the devil, who is the father of lies and therefore they hate the truth.

Three things come out of this passage:

Jesus is truth personified
Everything about Jesus as a person is trustworthy and true; he can be totally relied on. He is a safe guide for our lives. The rule of behaviour – 'what would Jesus do?' – is based on this.

Jesus' words are the truth.
Jesus words and promises are true; what he says can be totally relied upon. There are no lies or half-truths or anything misleading in what he says. We can stake our lives on his words.

Those who follow Jesus should love truth and hate lies
If we are to imitate Jesus then we should adopt his attitude to truth. In fact, as Jesus later says (John 16:13), one of the tasks of the Holy Spirit is to lead us into all truth.

We need to act

We need to repent of our abuse of the truth

We need to repent of our lies, our insinuations, half-truths, gossip and excuses.

We need to come to Jesus for cleansing

As we think about this commandment we will realise that we need forgiveness and cleansing. Jesus is the one who can wash us clean.

We need to resolve to live lives of truth in future

We need to determine that from now on we will speak the truth. This will take hard work and may be costly. It may require that we become accountable to someone who we can trust who will be 'speaking the truth in love' (Ephesians 4:15 NIV). They may be able to help us see what our sins of the tongue are.

We need to ask God for the power of the Holy Spirit to help us to live in the truth

We need to be aware that only the Spirit of truth working in our lives can enable us to triumph in the battle of truth and lies that we are engaged in.

We need to work at using our tongues for good not evil

Not only must we not testify falsely against our neighbour; we must speak the truth in love. It is not enough to avoid lying; we need to speak words that will build up and help.

All of us need to constantly work at being people whose words are true and good.

7) SUGGESTED PRAYERS
PRAYER OF CONFESSION

We live in a world full of words; radio, TV, books, posters, car stickers, newspapers, magazines, telephones, conversations, letters, e-mail and songs. Words are a great gift from God to us as humans. But as with all God's gifts we misuse them, using them selfishly, untruthfully, viciously, arrogantly and hurtfully. As we consider God's command that we should not bear false witness, we take time to consider the unwise way we use words.

> For the ease with which we twist the truth and speak falsely. Lord God of Truth forgive us.
> For the lies we tell to get ourselves off the hook. Lord God of Truth forgive us.
> For the gossip we have spread and delighted to hear. Lord God of Truth forgive us.
> For our unkind and hurtful words to those we love. Lord God of Truth forgive us.
> For the times we have not spoken up for others. Lord God of Truth forgive us.
> For the times we have been too quick to speak. Lord God of Truth forgive us.

We know the truth of your love, your forgiveness and your word. Clean our hearts so that our words please you. Fill us with your Holy Spirit that we might bear true witness in all we say and do. Amen.

PRAYER OF COMMITMENT

Holy God, we thank you that you are true in every way; indeed that you are truth itself. We thank you that by your word the Heavens and the Earth were created and are upheld. We thank you that Jesus Christ your son came to this Earth as the Word of God and in his life, teaching and actions showed that he was indeed the truth in human form. We thank you for his example to us. We thank you too that after Jesus returned to you he sent the Holy Spirit to guide his people into all truth.

We come before you and acknowledge that by our use of words we have sinned against you. Far too often we have lied to ourselves and to others, we have deceived people by what we have said, we have failed to tell the whole truth and we have used excuses or shared hurtful gossip. We confess that so much of what we have said has been wrong and is displeasing to you.

We repent of our words and of the intentions behind them. We come before the cross of Jesus Christ and ask for forgiveness and restoration. We bring to you those that we have hurt or deceived by our use of words and pray for healing for them. We ask that you would equip us through the power of the Holy Spirit to use words wisely. We ask that in the days ahead you use our words for good and not for evil.

We pray for ourselves that we would both love the truth and speak the truth. We pray that our words would be used for the building up of the body of Christ and not for its destruction.

We pray for our churches that they would be places of healing where we would be able to speak the truth in love to one another.

We pray for our society that it would be a society where truth is valued and where the lie is despised. We pray for those who govern our land that they would have honesty in what they say and that, honouring truth, they would be men and women of their word.

Finally, Lord God, help us to always deal with you in truth and help us to make the truth our guide in all our words and actions.

Through Jesus Christ our Lord, Amen.

Commandment 8: Exodus 20:17 'Do not steal.'

[Note: I think that with this topic particular care has to be exercised, to take into account the nature and setting of the listeners. To use exactly the same words and phrases to a group of rich City financiers and a congregation of struggling farmers would be thoughtless. Equally, great sensitivity needs to be taken in talking about employment, as in each gathering there may be people who, for various reasons, are not in paid work. In fact money is only part of the problem this commandment addresses; as I try to point out, stealing is about more than money. It is about how we use every part of our lives.]

1) SUGGESTED HYMNS & SONGS

HYMNS
- All creatures of our God and King
- King of glory, King of peace
- At the name of Jesus
- Now thank we all our God

SONGS
- No longer mine Lord but yours
- As the deer pants for the water
- Over all the earth you reign on high
- You resist the proud (High and lifted up)
- I will offer up my life
- I love you, Lord
- Justice and mercy [Matt Redman]

2) WARM-UP ACTIVITIES AND ILLUSTRATIONS

PARTICIPATORY QUESTIONS
Either
1) Ask what a thief looks like
[Note: You presumably will get the standard cartoon description of a man in dark clothes with a mask and a cloth cap and a sack over his shoulder.]

- Has anyone ever seen anybody dressed like this?
- So is there no stealing? Why did you lock your homes before coming into church?

2) Ask how many people in the church have been burgled?

- Can they remember their emotions when they discovered that they had been burgled? How did it make them feel?
- Did it change any of their attitudes to property?
- How many people fear being burgled – and if they do what does their fear make them do, and how differently does their fear cause them to act?

Or

1) Ask if there was no stealing then would things change in our lives? Who'd go out of business? *[Note: Insurance companies, police, security firms, etc.]*

2) What words do we use instead of 'steal'?
[Note: You might get 'nick', 'swipe', 'loan', 'acquire', 'borrow', 'filch', 'expropriate', 'commandeer', 'pilfer', 'made off with', 'pinch', 'lift', etc. There will probably be various dialect terms too.]

- Why are there so many different names?
- Why don't we simply just call it stealing or theft?

[Note: You should draw out that changing the words seems to make things less serious. People feel less guilty about 'acquiring' something than 'stealing' it.]

QUOTABLE FIGURES
In 1954 there were 75,443 reported burglaries in the UK. There are now over a million burglaries a year.

An income tax analysis reported 'precise statistics are impossible to obtain since no one knows the amount of income that escapes taxation through evasion, unrecorded financial transactions and other similar activities. Inland Revenue officials estimate that the amount is between £5,000 and £17,000 million a year.'

The Serious Fraud Office estimates that financial crime costs British companies around £29 billion annually.

3) CHILDREN'S ACTIVITY

There are two options here

Either

GUESSING AND GREED
Preparation

- Have twenty 10p coins arranged in a line so everyone can see them.
- Bottle of Tippex or indelible marker.
- You will need to know of a place that is well known to the children, that is about seventeen miles away from the church.

Activity

- Ask for a volunteer from among the children. Get them to put a mark on one coin with the Tippex or marker.

- Now get them to turn around so that they cannot see the coins. Put the marked coin into the line of coins and shuffle them about.
- Have the child try to guess which coin is the marked one.

[Note: The chances are very high that they will not guess it at one go. If they do, repeat the procedure.]

If you have the time and inclination you could either get another volunteer to try or give the first volunteer another chance to find the 10p.

Conclusion

It's not easy is it? Ask them how would they like to try and guess it in a line of coins seventeen miles long. You will probably have to give an illustration of how long this is in terms of real places.

They will say that it is impossible.

The punch line is that finding one 10p in seventeen miles of 10p's is more likely than winning the Lottery!

Question: So why do people do the Lottery?
Answer: Try to draw the answer that they hope to gain what is not theirs. *[Note: Quote for adults: 'A lottery is a tax on people who are bad at maths'.]*
Question: How else do people try to get what is not theirs to have?
Answer: Stealing or working.

- Many people live their lives hoping to gain what is not theirs. They are never happy.
- We are to be content with what we have. If we need more we are to work for it and earn it honestly.
- Gambling, stealing or working are all ways of getting money. The only way of getting money that God approves of is working, although it is not wrong to inherit something or be given it.

Or

WHO OWNS WHAT?
There are two possibilities here.

Either

CORPORATE IDENTITY

Preparation:
Collect pictures of as many recognisable corporate or government logos as you can and put them on overhead transparencies. You could try McDonalds, Michelin, Shell, Tommy Hilfiger, Mercedes, British Telecom, Wella, Warner Brothers, Renault, Body Shop, Volkswagen, Lloyds Bank, Powergen, Nike, Adidas, Barclays, Virgin, Coke, etc.

Activity
- Either divide the children into two teams and have a quiz to see which team can identify the most logos or just go over them one by one seeing who can guess them first.
- Ask people what the point of these logos is. Draw out that they either mark something as belonging to a company or organisation or as being made by that company.

Conclusion
If God had a logo what would he put it on? Draw out that God made and owns everything. So, who owns the whole world?

Or

LIBRARY BOOK

Preparation
Get a library book. Preferably old and of low value in case it all goes wrong.

Activity

Hiding the fact that it is a library book, show the children the book. Pretend that you are so fed up with it that you want to destroy it at the end of the service.

- Ask for ideas on how to destroy it.
- As you are discussing it let someone who is trustworthy (and literate!) glance at it. They ought to point out that it is a library book. [If not, prompt them.]
- Ask why you can't destroy it. [Hopefully, there will be a strong protest made that you can't do what you want with something that isn't yours.]
- Ask what will happen if you did burn it? [Hopefully, there will be the point made that it would be an offence and you would suffer a punishment.]

Conclusion

After making the point that we need to respect library books, point out that you can't do what you want with something that says 'Property of Someone Else' and that is only loaned to you. Go on to say that everything in the world (money, animals, people, air and water) belongs to God and that all that we have (for example, our lives, our money, our skills) are things that he has loaned to us. One day, when we die, God will ask for them back and we will have to explain what we did with them. We need to look after God's world carefully and have the right attitude to things.

4) BIBLE READINGS

The two suggested sets of readings are:

1) A compilation of Old Testament verses relevant to the theme of stealing, arranged for a number of readers.

2) Three New Testament passages arranged for a number of readers.

Both readings can be read straight by a single reader.

OLD TESTAMENT

CAST
Introducer: As before
Text Narrator: As before
8 Readers: Various voices.

Introducer: The Eighth Commandment says 'Do not steal'.

Text Narrator: In the Old Testament Book of Proverbs the prayer of a man called Agur is recorded.

Reader 1: O God, I beg two favours from you before I die. First, help me never to tell a lie. Second, give me neither poverty nor riches! Give me just enough to satisfy my needs. For if I grow rich, I may deny you and say, 'Who is the LORD?' And if I am too poor, I may steal and thus insult God's holy name.

(Proverbs 30:7–9)

Introducer: But what does it mean to steal?

Text Narrator: In the Book of Exodus God says this to his people:

Reader 2: If you lend money to a fellow Hebrew in need, do not be like a money lender, charging interest. If you take your neighbour's cloak as a pledge of repayment, you must return it by nightfall. Your neighbour will need it to stay warm during the night. If you do not return it and your neighbour cries out to me for help, then I will hear, for I am very merciful.

(Exodus 22:25–27)

Narrator: In the Book of Leviticus God says this to his people:

Reader 3: 'Do not cheat or rob anyone. Always pay your hired workers promptly... Do not use dishonest standards when measuring length, weight, or volume. Your scales and weights must be accurate. Your containers for measuring dry goods or liquids must be accurate.'

(Leviticus 19:13; 35–36)

Narrator: In the Book of Deuteronomy God says this to his people:

Reader 4: When you arrive in the land the LORD your God is giving you as a special possession, never steal someone's land by moving the boundary markers your ancestors set up to mark their property.

(Deuteronomy 19:14)

Narrator: God says to his people through the prophet Amos:

Reader 5: You trample the poor and steal what little they have through taxes and unfair rent. Therefore, you will never live in the beautiful stone houses you are building. You will never drink wine from the lush vineyards you are planting. For I know the vast number of your sins and rebellions. You oppress good people by taking bribes and deprive the poor of justice in the courts. So those who are wise will keep quiet, for it is an evil time. Do what is good and run from evil – that you may live! Then the LORD God Almighty will truly be your helper, just as you have claimed he is. Hate evil and love what is good; remodel your courts into true halls of justice. Perhaps even yet the LORD God Almighty will have mercy on his people who remain.

(Amos 5:11–15)

Narrator: And God says to his people, again through the prophet Amos:

Reader 6: Listen to this, you who rob the poor and trample the needy! You can't wait for the Sabbath day to be over and the religious festivals to end so you can get back to cheating the helpless. You measure out your grain in false measures and weigh it out on dishonest scales. And you mix the wheat you sell with chaff swept from the floor! Then you enslave poor people for a debt of one piece of silver or a pair of sandals.

(Amos 8:4–6)

Narrator: God says to his people through the prophet Isaiah:

Reader 7: Destruction is certain for the unjust judges, for those who issue unfair laws. They deprive the poor, the widows, and the orphans of justice. Yes, they rob widows and fatherless children!

(Isaiah 10:1–2)

Text Narrator: God says to his people through the prophet Malachi:

Reader 8: Should people cheat God? Yet you have cheated me! But you ask, 'What do you mean? When did we ever cheat you?' You have cheated me of the tithes and offerings due to me. You are under a curse, for your whole nation has been cheating me.

(Malachi 3:8–9)

NEW TESTAMENT
I suggest three passages: Luke 12:13–21, Luke 19:1–10 and Philippians 2:5–11.

Luke 12:13-21

CAST

Introducer: See Service One
Text Narrator: See Service One
Man: Moaning, angry
Jesus: See Service Two
Rich Farmer: At a distance from the others; perhaps at second microphone
God: Off-stage, a booming voice; the tone should perhaps be both that of condemnation and pity

Introducer: The New Testament talks about many people who were involved in giving or taking things. Jesus told the story of one man who was so hungry for things that he lost the most important thing that he had.

Text Narrator: Then someone called from the crowd to Jesus:

Man: Teacher, please tell my brother to divide our father's estate with me.

Jesus: Friend, who made me a judge over you to decide such things as that?

Text Narrator: Then Jesus said to the crowd:

Jesus: Beware! Don't be greedy for what you don't have. Real life is not measured by how much we own.

Text Narrator: And Jesus gave them this illustration:

Jesus: A rich man had a fertile farm that produced fine crops. In fact, his barns were full to overflowing. So he said:

Rich Farmer: I know! I'll tear down my barns and build bigger ones. Then I'll have room enough to store everything. And I'll sit back and say to myself, My friend, you have enough stored away for years to come. Now take it easy! Eat, drink, and be merry!

Jesus: But God said to him:

God: You fool! You will die this very night. Then who will get it all?

Jesus: Yes, a person is a fool to store up earthly wealth but not have a rich relationship with God.

(Luke 12:13–21)

Luke 19:1-10

CAST
Introducer
Text Narrator
Jesus: As in Service Two. Note that he ends with a very solemn pronouncement.
Zacchaeus: In just one line he has to give the impression of being repentant and joyful as a result of having met Jesus
Crowd: At least two people. Just one line but should be delivered with a grumbling and outraged tone.

Introducer: That was a man in a story. But there was also a real man who was wealthy – and corrupt – who met Jesus. His life changed as a result and the first thing that changed was his attitude to money. He was a tax collector for the Romans; they collected taxes from everywhere they conquered. To do it they appointed local men to get the taxes; it was an unpopular job but if you were ruthless and greedy you could make a lot of money.

Text Narrator: On his way to Jerusalem, Jesus entered Jericho and made his way through the town. There was a man there named Zacchaeus. He was one of the most influential Jews in the Roman tax-collecting business, and he had become very rich. He tried to get a look at Jesus, but he was too short to see over the crowds. So he ran ahead and climbed a sycamore tree beside the road, so he could watch from there. When Jesus came by, he looked up at Zacchaeus and called him by name.

Jesus: Zacchaeus! Quick, come down! For I must be a guest in your home today.

Text Narrator: Zacchaeus quickly climbed down and took Jesus to his house in great excitement and joy. But the crowds were displeased.

Crowd: He has gone to be the guest of a notorious sinner!

Text Narrator: Meanwhile, Zacchaeus stood there and said to the Lord...

Zacchaeus: I will give half my wealth to the poor, Lord. And if I have overcharged people on their taxes, I will give them back four times as much!

Jesus: Salvation has come to this home today, for this man has shown himself to be a son of Abraham. And I, the Son of Man, have come to seek and save those like him who are lost.

(Luke 19:1–10)

Philippians 2:5-11

CAST
Introducer: As above
Paul

Introducer: And the New Testament tells of a rich person, indeed someone who had the greatest possible riches, who gave everything away in order to do God's will. In his letter to the church in Philippi, the Apostle Paul writes as follows:

Paul: Don't be selfish; don't live to make a good impression on others. Be humble, thinking of others as better than yourself. Don't think only about your own affairs, but be interested in others, too, and what they are doing. Your attitude should be the same that Christ Jesus had. Though he was God, he did not demand and cling to his rights as God. He made himself nothing; he took the humble position of a slave and appeared in human form. And in human form he obediently humbled himself even further by dying a criminal's death on a cross. Because of this, God raised him up to the heights of heaven and gave him a name that is above every other name, so that at the name of Jesus every knee will bow, in heaven and on earth and under the earth, and every tongue will confess that Jesus Christ is Lord, to the glory of God the Father.

(Philippians 2:5–11)

5) POEM BY STEWART HENDERSON

Using reason, –
which, by the way,
is only on loan to you, –
you conclude that it is likely
that you will filch, swindle, loot,
fraud, lift, maraud.
(choose whichever slang or legal term
you deem appropriate)
Appropriate, that's another stolen word.

So, because of your tendency
to take things, possessions, tribal lands, hotel towels,
childhood, tiger's teeth, reputations, and so on,
you have come up with all manner of
gadgets, systems, and initiatives.
Initiative, that's something else that doesn't
belong to you.

So, let me remind you of just some
of your achievements –
burglar alarms, barristers, wigs, insurance
premiums, deposit boxes, Dobermans, handcuffs.

Battering rams, moats, boiling oil, missiles,
tracking systems, notices forbidding more than
two children in the shop at any time.

Tabloid fury, counselling for victims,
border guards, resistance movements, snipers,
closed circuit cameras, staff searches, immobilisers,
borstals, and Nick Ross.

Entry phones, alibis, combination locks,
PIN numbers, perspex till covers, customs posts,
and DNA.
That last item is not yours either
but you behave as though it belongs to you,
which technically is fraud.
In fact very little is yours,
if anything at all.

You say,
'Disobedience is profitable,
and deception is lucrative.'
You have accumulated much.
I hope that when, eventually,
committal proceedings commence,
you have an exceptional counsel for the defence.
You will need it.

6) SERMON

STEALING OR GIVING?

Commandment 8: Exodus 20:17 'Do not steal.'

Introduction
One of the interesting ways human beings have of dealing with
the Ten Commandments is by creating a mental image – a cari-
cature – of what someone who breaks the commandments looks
like. For example, we all think we know what a person who wor-
ships idols looks like; it is someone in a jungle bowing down in
worship before some stone or wood statue. And once we have
that mental image we can breathe a sigh of relief because that
isn't us. Now the way we handle 'you shall not steal' is reveal-
ing. We know what a thief is. It is a masked man (why is it
always a man?) dressed in black carrying a bag marked 'Swag' or
'Loot' over his shoulder. Now unless we are dressed like this, we
are not thieves. What good news!

We conceal things further by using other words to disguise
what we do. One man takes money from work and calls it 'bor-
rowing'; another woman cheats on her expenses and thinks of it
as 'just helping herself'; another man steals things from the
work store and talks about 'liberating them'. Very few of us can
stare at ourselves in a mirror and say 'I am a thief'. A thief is
someone who burgles houses, robs pensioners, breaks into cars.
Stealing is what someone else does.

Yet stealing is wider and broader than we like to think.
Stealing is to wrongfully take anything that does not belong to
you; with human sinfulness and ingenuity being what they are,
there are countless ways of doing this.

The many ways of stealing

Direct theft

The most obvious type of stealing is where something is just taken; what you could call 'good old-fashioned theft'. A purse vanishes, a car goes, a suitcase disappears, a till is emptied, a house is burgled. Of course it also occurs at a lower level, where it is somehow more acceptable. How many people take pens or paper from their employers? How many borrow equipment or use a firm's car for their private business? How many people steal from their employers by their misuse of phones, photocopiers or internet access?

Now we all know this sort of direct theft is wrong. The issue is that so often we do not imagine we are stealing; we think we are supplementing our income, or taking a souvenir, or enjoying a perk of the job. And, of course we say, everyone else is doing it. Such is our ability to deceive ourselves that even Christians can delude themselves that they are not stealing. In the Los Angeles riots of 1992 a reporter interviewed a man who had been one of a crowd of people who had looted a music store. When asked what he had stolen, the man replied, 'Gospel tapes. I love Jesus.'

What we need here is a ruthless mental honesty. We all need to evaluate before God everything that we do and ask of any remotely dubious practice; is this theft?

Fraud

Let me move on to the vast area of more subtle, indirect theft. Fraud is theft by deception. It is the unholy marriage of lying and theft; the result of simultaneously breaking the Eighth and Ninth commandments.

We think of fraud as being a modern speciality and it is true that we have more ways of doing it than ever before. We have false accounts, fake documents, inflated budgets, misleading advertisements and so on. Yet fraud is just another form of theft.

It is plainly condemned in the Old Testament. Moving

boundary stones was one way of increasing your estate and is described as stealing in Deuteronomy 19:14 ('When you arrive in the land the LORD your God is giving you as a special possession, never steal someone's land by moving the boundary markers your ancestors set up to mark their property'). When the land was a family's source of food and wealth, the loss of even a small strip of land could make the difference between life or death.

Another way to defraud people was to have bogus weights, have misleading measuring containers or to water down or dilute what you sold. Hear what the prophet Amos says: 'Listen to this, you who rob the poor and trample the needy! You can't wait for the Sabbath day to be over and the religious festivals to end so you can get back to cheating the helpless. You measure out your grain in false measures and weigh it out on dishonest scales. And you mix the wheat you sell with chaff swept from the floor! Then you enslave poor people for a debt of one piece of silver or a pair of sandals' (Amos 8:4–6).

The thrust of the Old Testament here (and in the other verses we have read) is on the human cost of stealing. In the passages we read earlier you may have noticed the references to robbing the poor, the widows and orphans and those who are defenceless. God cares for such people and God is angry when we cheat them.

Fraud is easy to slip into because it is a 'clean', almost respectable crime. You don't have to mug old ladies, break into houses or walk out through checkouts with things hidden under your jacket. You keep your hands dirt-free. Yet it is still theft from someone. Few people would directly steal hospital equipment but many people would not blink at cheating the Inland Revenue of the money that might be used to buy hospital equipment. The effects are the same.

Again, we need to look at our lives to see if there is anything in them that fits this. Are we involved personally in selling or marketing anything that is not exactly what it says it is? When someone pays us for our work do they get what they paid for? Are we ever guilty of providing a sub-standard service? And, bearing in mind the Old Testament's references to the vulnerable in society, do we have the same standard for the poor and helpless as we do for the rich and influential? Do we distinguish between private and public customers?

In God's eyes fraud, however subtle, is still theft.

Exploitation

Another way of stealing from people that is condemned in the Bible is any form of exploitation. For example, Leviticus 19:13 ('Do not cheat or rob anyone. Always pay your hired workers promptly.') says that wages are to be paid promptly. Two interesting rules about loans are given in Exodus 22:25–27 ('If you lend money to a fellow Hebrew in need, do not be like a money lender, charging interest. If you take your neighbour's cloak as a pledge of repayment, you must return it by nightfall. Your neighbour will need it to stay warm during the night. If you do not return it and your neighbour cries out to me for help, then I will hear, for I am very merciful.') One was that loans to fellow Israelites were to be interest-free. The second was that whatever a lender took from a borrower as a guarantee of repayment of a loan was not to cause them actual need. However these rules are to be applied today, the point is clear; people who needed money were to be mercifully treated.

Other areas of exploitation and social injustice are addressed elsewhere in the Old Testament. Isaiah 10:1–2 ('Destruction is certain for the unjust judges, for those who issue unfair laws. They deprive the poor, the widows, and the orphans of justice. Yes, they rob widows and fatherless children!') deals with exploitation of people by the use of an unfair legal system. And Amos 5:10–11 ('How you hate honest judges! How you despise people who tell the truth! You trample the poor and steal what little they have through taxes and unfair rent.') covers stealing from the poor by high taxes and rent.

Now in Old Testament times the focus of the prophets was on their own nation and on the people immediately around them. Our modern world has wider horizons. Our government is involved in decisions that affect the whole world; the banks we use and the firms we work for may have enormous influence on people thousands of miles from us.

Much as we would prefer otherwise, we are all linked in with national and global effects. We ourselves may not be directly involved in imposing taxes, setting rents or even making loans. But we are indirectly involved by who we vote into power, by which companies we support, by whose pension funds we subscribe to or even by what we buy at a supermarket.

If we are involved directly in decisions on rent, wages and loans we need to be aware that God will hold us responsible for how we use – or abuse – our powers. Even if we are not directly involved in such decisions then we need to use our power as voters, subscribers or shareholders to work for justice.

Subtle stealing

When you look closely at the idea of stealing you realise how many ways there are of robbing people of what is theirs. We can for instance rob other people of time. A workaholic father might be stealing from his family, time he should be spending with them. A wife who is a sports fanatic might steal from her husband time they should be having together.

Another form of stealing is damaging the environment. By destroying the countryside or making a species extinct, by polluting the air and the water, aren't we robbing our children of their inheritance?

It is even possible to rob God. This is spelt out in Malachi 3:8–9 ('Will a man rob God? Yet you rob me.' But you ask, 'How do we rob you?' 'In tithes and offerings. You are under a curse – the whole nation of you – because you are robbing me.'). We have duties and obligations to God and it is all too easy to cheat him; to not give him what we owe.

These raise issues about what stealing is and why it is wrong. Clearly it is more than money and things; so what is it?

Why is stealing wrong?

We have looked at the different types of stealing; but what is it that lies behind them? What is it that is at the core of the whole sin of theft? Is it just that stealing is just wrong? Or is it that we ought to respect the possessions of others?

Let me give you three reasons why stealing is wrong.

Theft is an offence against God

The heart of the whole problem of stealing is the belief that things are ours and that they belong to us so that we can do we want with them. But if we think that, then we have misunderstood the whole nature of this world. In fact nothing is really ours; it is all God's. Psalm 24:1 summarises the situation: 'The earth is the LORD's, and everything in it, the world, and all who live in it.'

It is as if everything in this world, everything from plants and birds to houses and banknotes, has invisibly inscribed on it 'Property of God'. Whenever we are given something, whether it is wages or a gift, God holds us accountable for it. It is as if in heaven there are ledger books (or database files if you are computer literate!) in which, against our name, is the full list of what we have been given. These items are those things that have been entrusted to us. What we have is loaned to us, not owned by us.

So absolutely everything we have, is issued by God on temporary loan to us. This is spelt out in Matthew 25:14–30:

> Again, the Kingdom of Heaven can be illustrated by the story of a man going on a trip. He called together his servants and gave them money to invest for him while he was gone. He gave five bags of gold to one, two bags of gold to another, and one bag of gold to the last – dividing it in proportion to their abilities – and then left on his trip. The servant who received the five bags of gold began immediately to invest the money and soon doubled it. The servant with two bags of gold also went right to work and doubled the money. But the servant who received the one bag of gold

dug a hole in the ground and hid the master's money for safekeeping. After a long time their master returned from his trip and called them to give an account of how they had used his money. The servant to whom he had entrusted the five bags of gold said, 'Sir, you gave me five bags of gold to invest, and I have doubled the amount.' The master was full of praise. 'Well done, my good and faithful servant. You have been faithful in handling this small amount, so now I will give you many more responsibilities. Let's celebrate together!'

Next came the servant who had received the two bags of gold, with the report, 'Sir, you gave me two bags of gold to invest, and I have doubled the amount.' The master said, 'Well done, my good and faithful servant. You have been faithful in handling this small amount, so now I will give you many more responsibilities. Let's celebrate together!'

Then the servant with the one bag of gold came and said, 'Sir, I know you are a hard man, harvesting crops you didn't plant and gathering crops you didn't cultivate. I was afraid I would lose your money, so I hid it in the earth and here it is.'

But the master replied, 'You wicked and lazy servant! You think I'm a hard man, do you, harvesting crops I didn't plant and gathering crops I didn't cultivate? Well, you should at least have put my money into the bank so I could have some interest. Take the money from this servant and give it to the one with the ten bags of gold. To those who use well what they are given, even more will be given, and they will have an abundance. But from those who are unfaithful, even what little they have will be taken away. Now throw this useless servant into outer darkness, where there will be weeping and gnashing of teeth.'

The point is this, whatever God gives us, he expects us to use wisely. So how does this affect the issue of stealing? The answer is simple and sobering. When we steal we don't just steal from some other person or from the government; we steal from God himself.

In Psalm 51, the psalm where David confesses to his adultery with Bathsheba and the murder of her husband, Uriah, he says something that at first strikes us as odd. In verse 4 he says to God, 'Against you, and you alone, have I sinned; I have done what is evil in your sight.'

I think that what David is acknowledging here is this: although he sinned against Bathsheba and Uriah, ultimately his sin was against God. They belonged to him and because of that, David's adultery with Bathsheba and murder of Uriah, are crimes against God.

When we think about stealing we need to remember that who we steal from, ultimately, is God, himself. And God sees.

Stealing betrays our relationship to God

If we have come to faith in Christ then we have become a son or daughter of God and God has become our Heavenly Father.

This has at least two implications for stealing. First, we are to trust our Heavenly Father for what we need. If we need something that we cannot get by working, we are to pray for it. To steal something is to reject the idea that God our Father knows best what we really need. It is actually an act of rebellion; it is saying to him that we know best.

Secondly, God expects us, as his children, to reflect his character. We are to bear the family likeness. Time and time again the Old Testament prophets talk about the justice of God; how he is a good, merciful, just and loving God. His children are to be like him. He doesn't turn a blind eye to exploitation or to injustice and neither should we.

To be a thief is to deny that God is our Father or that we are his children.

Stealing is bad for us

Finally, God is against stealing because stealing is bad for us. Again, we need to be reminded that the Ten Commandments are not severe rules made by a tough God who wants to put his people through impossible tests. They are instructions made by our Creator so that we can live and prosper.

For one thing, stealing is bad for us as a community. Stealing means lying and it inevitably produces anger, division and mistrust. It is impossible for God's people to live in the way that he expects if there is stealing from each other.

For another thing it is bad for us as individuals. It leads to deception and lies and it starts a vicious circle where we want more so we end up stealing even more. The thief who is caught because he or she gets too greedy is a common phenomenon.

Theft also has eternal consequences. In I Corinthians 6:10, Paul explicitly says that thieves will not share in the Kingdom of God. If you or I claim to be a Christian and consistently steal, we must question whether we are indeed born again of God's Spirit or whether we are deluding ourselves. In fact I would go further; if you or I claim to be a Christian and show no spirit of generosity, no desire to give, then we must examine ourselves carefully.

There is also another and more positive side to how we deal with things. We learn from Jesus' teaching in the Gospels that God is interested in how we have been stewards of what he has given us in this life. In Luke 16:10–12 we read that 'Unless you are faithful in small matters, you won't be faithful in large ones. If you cheat even a little, you won't be honest with greater responsibilities. And if you are untrustworthy about worldly wealth, who will trust you with the true riches of heaven? And if you are not faithful with other people's money, why should you be trusted with money of your own?' How we handle our resources – and those of other people – in this life is going to determine what we are entrusted with for all eternity!

Our response

Let me suggest, in considering this commandment not to steal, that four responses are appropriate.

Reflection

We need to think over our attitude to possessions. We need to remember that God is the source of all things; that all we possess is a temporary loan from God and that we have no right to possessions. It is far too easy to get our priorities for our lives from the media rather than from God and his word.

Repentance

As a result of our reflections, we may easily feel that we have sinned in this area. We need to say sorry to God and to resolve to live lives that are marked by the wise use of God's gifts in the future. We need to set out God's standards in our lives and be determined to live by them.

Restitution

Linked with repentance comes restitution. Stealing is one of the few sins where we can make amends. If we have committed theft then returning or repaying what was stolen is essential. The passage we read about Zacchaeus makes the point; in his case he was so overjoyed to be accepted by Jesus that he went well beyond what was strictly needed to make restitution. But in making amends it never hurts to err on the generous side.

In situations where revival occurs, widespread restitution can be spectacular. When Rev. W. P. Nicholson preached in Belfast in the 1920s so many shipyard workers were spiritually convicted of the sin of theft that the main firm there had to build a new shed to hold all the returned items.

Realignment

As elsewhere with the Ten Commandments we need to look hard at our own lives and realign them according to God's word.

- We should be grateful for what we have. We need to continually remind ourselves that everything that we have is a loan from God, for which one day we will be held accountable for, as to how we got it and how we used it. We must learn to thank God for his gifts rather than to seek what is not ours to have.

- We must act justly. Micah 6:8 says that God requires us to 'do what is right, to love mercy, and to walk humbly with your God'. We need to live for God in every area of our lives.

- We need to use wisely what God has given us. In the story of the servants entrusted with riches by their master, Jesus makes the point that doing nothing with what we have is not an option. We need to use what he has given, to make it bear fruit. In particular we need to encourage stewardship. The answer to so many of the world's problems, from the environmental crisis to global poverty, lies in applying the concept that we are stewards accountable to God. We live on this Earth not because we own it but because God has allowed us to share in it. We are tenants not owners, and as such we need to realise that we have no right to do what we want with God's world. We need to be wise managers of the world's resources.

- We must give generously. It is clear from the Bible that we steal not only by taking but by withholding. There are not only sins where we commit wrong things but also sins where we omit to do good things. Paul in Ephesians 4:28 gives a helpful ruling: 'If you are a thief, stop stealing. Begin using your hands for honest work, and then give generously to others in need.' The thief is not merely to give up stealing but also to adopt a new outlook and lifestyle marked by generosity not greed. Generosity, it has to be said, deals with more than money; it involves sharing time, energy, enthusiasm and other gifts.

Finally, the model for how we are to live is found in Jesus Christ. As we read in Philippians Chapter 2, Jesus' attitude was such that he did not even choose to grasp onto what were his rights as God. Instead, he willingly gave up everything in order to become human and to become one of us.

Let us close by hearing again Paul's words from Philippians 2:

Don't be selfish; don't live to make a good impression on others. Be humble, thinking of others as better than yourself. Don't think only about your own affairs, but be interested in others, too, and what they are doing. Your attitude should be the same that Christ Jesus had. Though he was God, he did not demand and cling to his rights as God. He made himself nothing; he took the humble position of a slave and appeared in human form. And in human form he obediently humbled himself even further by dying a criminal's death on a cross. Because of this, God raised him up to the heights of heaven and gave him a name that is above every other name, so that at the name of Jesus every knee will bow, in heaven and on earth and under the earth, and every tongue will confess that Jesus Christ is Lord, to the glory of God the Father.

Let us all live like Christ.

7) SUGGESTED PRAYERS

PRAYER OF CONFESSION
God of creation, the earth is yours
with all its beauty and goodness,
its rich and overflowing provision.

But we have claimed it for our own,
plundered its beauty for profit,
grabbed its resources for ourselves.

God of creation, forgive us.
May we no longer abuse your trust,
but act gently and with justice for your earth.

[Jan Berry, in Bread of Tomorrow, *ed. Janet Morley]*

Or

PRAYER OF CONFESSION AND COMMITMENT
Holy God, we acknowledge that you are a gracious and generous God who has given us so many good things. We thank you for your many good gifts to us. We confess that all that we have; wealth, life, friends and possessions, have come to us freely from you.

Father God, we reflect on all we have. We acknowledge that all we possess is a temporary loan from you. We remind ourselves that, as you have given, so you have a right to take away and that one day all that we have will be taken from us. Furthermore, we acknowledge that one day we will be called to account for the way we have used what you have given us. We pray that the knowledge that we are accountable to you would govern our use of all your gifts to us. We acknowledge that we have no rights to anybody else's property. We ask that you would give us a spirit of contentment so that we would be grateful to you for those things that we do have instead of continually seeking for things that we do not have. Help us to be content to have our needs met rather than to continually seek to have our wants fulfilled.

Father God, we come to you in repentance. We confess that in many different ways we have been people who have stolen. We have taken things that are not ours and we have been selfish over what we have. We have taken rather than given. We confess our sins and pray that through our Lord Jesus Christ you would forgive us. We ask Lord that you would sharpen our consciences so that we would be able to see clearly through all the many temptations there are to steal. Grant us that when we are faced with wrong desires we would, through the power of your Holy Spirit, be enabled to resist.

Father God, we come to you in order that you might help us to make restitution. Help us, Lord, to examine our lives in the light of your teaching and under the scrutiny of your Holy Spirit who searches our hearts and minds. Where we realise that we have stolen things we ask you to show us how we can make restitution and make amends for what we have done.

Father God, we come to you asking that you realign our lives. Show us, O Lord, how to live lives that are free from a desire to take what is not ours to have. We ask instead that our lives might be marked by a rich generosity. As your children we pray that we would show something of your gracious love and forgiving spirit. We ask that we would be those who give as richly as you have given to us.

In all things help us to have the attitude of Jesus Christ who became poor for our sake.

May your name, Father, Son and Holy Spirit, be glorified in our lives. Amen.

Don't Commit Adultery!

Commandment 7: Exodus 20:14 'Do not commit adultery'.

*[Note: It ought to go without saying that to preach on adultery is to
walk through a minefield. Come down a fraction too hard and you
will offend people. Come down too a fraction too gentle and you will
have complaints that you are soft-peddling on the unequivocal
demands of Scripture. You need to prayerfully and thoughtfully consider what you are going to say. Nevertheless there is probably no area
of life where we more urgently need to hear God's word preached than
this.]*

1) SUGGESTED HYMNS AND SONG

HYMNS
- O Jesus I have promised
- Great is thy faithfulness
- Take my life and let it be (either the traditional or the
  Jubilate Hymns version)
- O worship the Lord
- Holy, holy, holy, Lord God Almighty

SONGS
- No longer mine Lord but yours
- Faithful One
- Purify my heart
- Can I ascend the hill of the Lord
- Jesus, you are changing me

- Pure pure heart [Matt Redman]
- The eyes of my heart [Matt Redman]

2) WARM-UP ACTIVITIES AND ILLUSTRATIONS

ACTIVITY

Bring out a gift-wrapped box of chocolates. Say they are a special present for your mother/father or your wife/husband *[Note: Whoever it is ought to be absent from the service]*, that they are her favourites and that it's a special occasion. Unwrap it, open the box and offer them around. There ought to be protests. Say 'it's no problem really' or 'she's very easy-going'. Then put the box back in its wrappings.

Ask why people were surprised by this.

You should be able to draw out that we consider private gifts something that we do not let other people have. Point out that if we are offended by this, how much more should we be offended by the abuse of a sexual relationship within marriage.

ILLUSTRATIONS

Christians believe that there is something wrong with the human race. If you wanted to prove this then it would be easy to do in the area of sex and marriage. For instance; there is the continual preoccupation with sex. This is used to sell everything from lawnmowers to pet food. [You can give illustrations; use recent newspaper or magazine cuttings.]

Yet despite the endless bombardment about sex there is a great deal of unhappiness in this area. Take for instance, marriage. Think of the following quips.

- 'When a newly married man looks happy, we know why. But when a ten-year married man looks happy, we wonder why.'
- 'Marriage is a three-ring circus: engagement ring, wedding ring, and suffering.'
- 'Marriage isn't a word, it's a sentence.'

Cynicism on marriage can be found in strange places. The following are allegedly genuine answers to Bible quiz questions.

- The seventh commandment is thou shalt not admit adultery.
- The epistles were the wives of the apostles.
- St Paul cavorted to Christianity. He preached holy acrimony which is another name for marriage.
- A Christian should have only one spouse. This is called monotony.

And it isn't just jokes. However you look at it, marriage in Britain is in trouble. The numbers of marriages are down and successful marriages are fewer. Nearly half of all marriages in England and Wales will end in divorce if the current rate is maintained. Yet no alternative has been invented. Cohabitations are even more likely to break down. Other trends are even more depressing:

Teenage pregnancies and cases of sexually transmitted diseases continue to rise. Sexual crime rises every year. Four times more rapes have been reported to the police in the last decade, but the number of convicted rapists has gone down from 24% to 9%. In 1996 half of all sexual assaults were from people in 'intimate relationships'.

Sex has been taken out of the context of a loving, secure, selfless relationship. What once was used as an expression of being united with one person forever, has now become, for many, little more than an erotic aerobics class. Magazines aimed at sixteen-year-olds have slots such as Position of the Month and their columns are filled with discussion about sex and sexuality.

Clearly we are getting something wrong here.

3) CHILDREN'S ACTIVITY

WHY WE NEED RULES
[Aims: To point out, using an illustration about flying, that most of the good things in life need rules attached to them or we get into seri-

ous trouble. Sex is no different. Note: In using the example of air travel do remember that, despite what some people think, not everybody flies abroad. Don't assume that every child has flown in a plane; those that haven't may feel excluded.]

PREPARATION
- Need two very cheap, fragile model planes; should look like airliners rather than fighters. Will be (hopefully!) damaged by illustration.
- Using a few sheets of paper make two short and narrow runways, one visible on a table at the front and the other at the back.

Start by carefully putting the planes at either end of the runway at the front.

ACTIVITY
Question: Who has flown a long way on a plane?
Question: If there were no planes then how would you have got there?
[Note: Presumably it would have taken days or weeks by sea or rail.]
Conclude that planes are a good thing.

- Announce that you are going to play airlines. Need two volunteers to run an airline each. Choose two competitive, aggressive and very mobile children.
- Have each child come to the front. Stress that the planes are full of people and have to be careful. Have to take off, fly to the end of the room, land, count twenty (for people to get off and on) and come back and land.
- Let them start off on the count of three. Inevitably it will become a race and there will be jostling; all being well the planes will collide.
- Reward both!

CONCLUSION

Question: We had no rules and what happened – or nearly happened?

Answer: A crash.

Question: Can a plane just fly anywhere it wants?

Answer: Draw out that you need rules or else you will have a crash. In fact planes fly by strict rules and also have to obey air traffic controllers. Explain; and illustrate by accounts of waiting to take off, etc.

Now there are lots of things in life that have rules to avoid disasters. Cars, electricity, adventure playgrounds, etc. Good things but they can prove dangerous if the rules are broken.

Now, God made men and women for each other so they are attracted to each other and want to spend their lives together. *[Note: Obviously, you alone are the best judge of how frank you can be here.]* Now this is good but to protect us from disaster he also created firm rules for how this is to happen. We have rules in the Bible that set out the only safe route; that is marriage. If you go off that route you get into trouble and you need to get back on course. God's Spirit is the equivalent of the Air Traffic Controller and gives us guidance.

4) BIBLE READINGS

The suggested readings are two passages from the Old Testament and two from the New. Other possible scripture passages are given at the end of this section.

OLD TESTAMENT
Genesis 2:8–25

CAST
Introducer
Text Narrator
Introducer: In the first pages of the Bible, God sets out his pattern for the human race

Text Narrator: And the LORD God said, 'It is not good for the man to be alone. I will make a companion who will help him.' So the LORD God formed from soil every kind of animal and bird. He brought them to Adam to see what he would call them, and Adam chose a name for each one. He gave names to all the livestock, birds, and wild animals. But still there was no companion suitable for him. So the LORD God caused Adam to fall into a deep sleep. He took one of Adam's ribs and closed up the place from which he had taken it. Then the LORD God made a woman from the rib and brought her to Adam. 'At last!' Adam exclaimed. 'She is part of my own flesh and bone! She will be called "woman", because she was taken out of a man.' This explains why a man leaves his father and mother and is joined to his wife, and the two are united into one. Now, although Adam and his wife were both naked, neither of them felt any shame.

Introducer: Yet within a page we read how the man and the woman rebelled against God. Every area of our human life was affected by their rebellion. One area that was badly distorted was the way that men and women relate to each other.

2 Samuel 11:1–27

CAST

Introducer
Text Narrator
Reader: Reads two minor parts
David: A fundamentally good man brought down into sin; not a natural rogue
Uriah: A man of great loyalty and integrity
Joab: A cynical, crafty warrior

Introducer: Almost as if to make the point about how vulnerable we are in the area of our sexuality, the Old Testament records how it was here that one of the greatest men of the Old Testament, David the psalm-writer, warrior and king, fell badly.

[Note: In some churches people may feel happier to omit the reference in verse 4 to Bathsheba having just had her period. This can be done but the writer presumably put it there to explain why David couldn't just pass the child off as Uriah's.]

Text Narrator: The following spring, the time of year when kings go to war, King David sent Joab and the Israelite army to destroy the Ammonites. In the process they laid siege to the city of Rabbah. But David stayed behind in Jerusalem. Late one afternoon David got out of bed after taking a nap and went for a stroll on the roof of the palace. As he looked out over the city, he noticed a woman of unusual beauty taking a bath. He sent someone to find out who she was, and he was told

Reader: She is Bathsheba, the daughter of Eliam and the wife of Uriah the Hittite.

Text Narrator: Then David sent for her; and when she came to the palace, he slept with her. *[She had just completed the purification rites after having her menstrual period.]* Then she returned home. Later, when Bathsheba discovered that she was pregnant, she sent a message to inform David. So David sent a message to Joab...

David: Send me Uriah the Hittite.

Text Narrator: When Uriah arrived, David asked him how Joab and the army were getting along and how the war was progressing. Then he told Uriah:

David: Go on home and relax. *[Note: there ought to be a distinct sexual innuendo here.]*

Text Narrator: David even sent a gift to Uriah after he had left the palace. But Uriah wouldn't go home. He stayed that night at the palace entrance with some of the king's other servants. When David heard what Uriah had done, he summoned him...

David: What's the matter with you? Why didn't you go home last night after being away for so long?

Uriah: The Ark and the armies of Israel and Judah are living in tents, and Joab and his officers are camping in the open fields. How could I go home to wine and dine and sleep with my wife? I swear that I will never be guilty of acting like that.

David: Well, stay here tonight, and tomorrow you may return to the army.

Text Narrator: So Uriah stayed in Jerusalem that day and the next. Then David invited him to dinner and got him drunk. But even then he couldn't get Uriah to go home to his wife. Again he slept at the palace entrance. So the next morning David wrote a letter to Joab and gave it to Uriah to deliver. In the letter David wrote...

David: Station Uriah on the front lines where the battle is fiercest. Then pull back so that he will be killed.

Text Narrator: So Joab assigned Uriah to a spot close to the city wall where he knew the enemy's strongest men were fighting. And Uriah was killed along with several other Israelite soldiers. Then Joab sent a battle report to David. He told his messenger...

Joab: Report all the news of the battle to the king. But he might get angry and ask, 'Why did the troops go so close to the city? Didn't they know there would be shooting from the walls? Wasn't Gideon's son Abimelech killed at Thebez by a woman who threw a millstone down on him?' Then tell him, 'Uriah the Hittite was killed, too.'

Text Narrator: So the messenger went to Jerusalem and gave a complete report to David.

Reader: The enemy came out against us. And as we chased them back to the city gates, the archers on the wall shot arrows at us. Some of our men were killed, including Uriah the Hittite.

David: Well, tell Joab not to be discouraged. The sword kills one as well as another! Fight harder next time, and conquer the city!

Text Narrator: When Bathsheba heard that her husband was dead, she mourned for him. When the period of mourning was over, David sent for her and brought her to the palace, and she became one of his wives. Then she gave birth to a son. But the LORD was very displeased with what David had done.

(2 Samuel 11:1–27)

Introducer: So David, the man of God, fell into lust, adultery, lying and, in the end, murder. We read that David repented of his sin and was forgiven by God but the repercussions of his sin were to hang over him all the days of his life.

NEW TESTAMENT
Matthew 5:27–30 and Ephesians 5:21–33

CAST
Introducer: See comments above
Jesus: See comments above
Paul

Introducer: Although Jesus was a single man, he strongly supported marriage. He re-emphasised the pattern God had given in Adam and Eve of lifelong marriage between one man and one woman, he attended weddings and wedding parties, he opposed the habits of easy divorce that had grown up in Israel, he refused to allow women to be treated as second-class citizens and he offered forgiveness to those who had committed sexual sin. But he also spoke out, not only against adultery, but also against the thoughts and desires that lay behind it. In Matthew 5 we read that he said this:

Jesus: You have heard that the law of Moses says, 'Do not commit adultery.' But I say, anyone who even looks at a woman with lust in his eye has already committed adultery with her in his heart. So if your eye – even if it is your good eye – causes you to lust, gouge it out and throw it away. It is better for you to lose one part of your body than for your whole body to be thrown into hell. And if your hand – even if it is your stronger hand – causes you to sin, cut it off and throw it away. It is better for you to lose one part of your body than for your whole body to be thrown into hell.

(Matthew 5:27–30)

Introducer: In his Letter to the Ephesians the apostle Paul spelt out why marriage was special; it was, he said, because the unity between the husband and wife was a picture of how Christ loved the church.

Paul: And further, you will submit to one another out of reverence for Christ. You wives will submit to your husbands as you do to the Lord. For a husband is the head of his wife as Christ is the head of his body, the church; he gave his life to be her Saviour. As the church submits to Christ, so you wives must submit to your husbands in everything. And you husbands must love your wives with the same love Christ showed the church. He gave up his life for her to make her holy and clean, washed by baptism and God's word. He did this to present her to himself as a glorious church without a spot or wrinkle or any other blemish. Instead, she will be holy and without fault. In the same way, husbands ought to love their wives as they love their own bodies. For a man is actually loving himself when he loves his wife. No one hates his own body but lovingly cares for it, just as Christ cares for his body, which is the church. And we are his body. As the Scriptures say, 'A man leaves his father and mother and is joined to his wife, and the two are united into one.' This is a great mystery, but it is an illustration of the way Christ and the church are one. So again I say, each man must love his wife as he loves himself, and the wife must respect her husband.

(Ephesians 5:21-33)

OTHER POSSIBLE PASSAGES
- Mark 10:6–9
- Hebrews 13:4
- Titus 2:11–12
- Philippians 4:8

5) POEM BY STEWART HENDERSON

> **How great was our garden**
> **how teeming its shoots**
> **how blazing its blossom**
> **how melting its fruits**
>
> **How vivid its fauna**
> **how subtle its shades**
> **Its mystery ocean**
> **and bronze esplanades**

How fertile its timbers
how placid its beasts
how gilded its stairways
how stately its feasts

How tender its mornings
how countless its moons
Its marble escarpments
and jasmine lagoons

Its Eros aromas
its primula nights
its quarter-tones birdsong
its infinite heights

But love's wedding carriage
is now a bleak hearse –
Indifference is painful
betrayal's far worse

My sacred beloved,
you left me to grieve
You're in bed with others,
Oh, Adam. Oh, Eve.

6) SERMON

[Note: Trying to cover all topics to do with sex, marriage and adultery here is not only quite impossible it is probably pastorally disastrous. Divorce is a major issue today and there will, of course, be people in any gathering who have been divorced. My experience is that issues such as these are best addressed in a face-to-face and private pastoral meeting.]

ADULTERY OR FAITHFULNESS?

Commandment 7: Exodus 20:14 'Do not commit adultery.'

INTRODUCTION

One reason people give as to why they don't like formal Christianity is that 'it tells you what you can and cannot do'. Instinctively, as soon as we hear a 'do not' we tend to react as if our freedom is being curtailed. But it is vital to remember that there are two sorts of commands. Some commands are for the benefit of the person issuing the orders: 'Get me a cup of tea', 'Get out of my way' and 'March around the block'. Other commands are for our good: 'Stand clear of doors', 'Stop at red light', 'Switch electricity off at wall before opening case'.

Now I believe that God's commands on sex are of the second kind; they have been given for our best interest. The children's illustration about flying planes is actually quite profound. There are thick rule-books for pilots on when, where and how they are to fly planes with hundreds of people in them and there is a network of air traffic controllers and strictly marked out flight paths because it is only with such restrictions that flying is safe. God's rules on sex serve the same purpose; they are to allow us to enjoy life without sex destroying us.

Now of course you really ought to have a series of sermons on sex. After all, it's a large topic. What about homosexual temptation? What about remarriage of divorcees? What about being single? What about sex within marriage? Here I simply want to mention four things that seem to me to lie at the heart of the Bible's teaching on sex and marriage. They are also the areas where big lies have been told.

THE VALUE OF SEX

There are so many beliefs about sex, some of them dangerously wrong, that we need to understand what the Bible says about the subject. We need to have God's perspective on the matter.

In fact sex is discussed right at the start of the Bible. In

Genesis 1 and 2 we read how God created man and woman for each other so that there could be relationship and partnership. What's more in Genesis 1:28 he commands Adam and Eve 'Have sex!'. Now it doesn't actually say that; it just says that God 'blessed them and told them, "Multiply and fill the earth and subdue it."' But in order to multiply you do have to have sex! So God is behind sex; he invented it.

However from these early chapters of Genesis we learn something more about the nature of the context in which God designed sex. When Adam first claps his eyes on Eve he says 'At last! She is part of my own flesh and bone!' and the writer comments, 'This explains why a man leaves his father and mother and is joined to his wife, and the two are united into one. Now, although Adam and his wife were both naked, neither of them felt any shame.'

What we see in this passage is the foundations of marriage as God planned it. Here there are three key things – ingredients if you like – that are essential for a marriage relationship. The three phrases here are 'leaving', 'joining' and 'being united into one'. The older King James version memorably had it that 'Therefore shall a man leave his father and his mother, and shall cleave unto his wife: and they shall be one flesh.'

- Leaving: The man and the woman cease to be under their parent's authority. Instead they start a family of their own, a new social unit. This speaks of the legal, economic and social elements of marriage. Until the day of marriage, both bride and groom would have been members of their parent's households and under their parent's authority. Now they start a household of their own.
- Joining or cleaving: This speaks of an embracing of the other person in every area of their lives and refers to the uniting of the couple so that they now have a personal and emotional oneness. The old word 'cleave' here means to stick together (the word 'clay' comes from the same root).

- Being united into one or being one flesh: This refers to the physical act of uniting bodies. As the woman was made out of the man so, by the sexual act, she and he are reunited physically. This act of uniting bodies is seen as far more than a simple physical togetherness. It is a uniting of all that we are emotionally and psychologically.

What this passage teaches (and it is so important that both Jesus and Paul quote it) is that in human beings the sexual act was designed to be a key part of the marriage bond between husband and wife. It cannot be separated from the context of a stable marriage.

Sex is something that has been distorted by what we call the Fall; the act of disobedience of Adam and Eve that affected them and all human beings since.

The high worth of sex and marriage are shown in other passages in the Bible. For instance, one whole book of the Old Testament, the Song of Songs, is a series of love poems. Similar language about sex is found in the Book of Proverbs, 'Let your wife be a fountain of blessing for you. Rejoice in the wife of your youth. She is a loving doe, a graceful deer. Let her breasts satisfy you always. May you always be captivated by her love. Why be captivated, my son, with an immoral woman, or embrace the breasts of an adulterous woman?' (Proverbs 5:18–20.)

There are other illustrations of God's high estimate of sex. In the Book of Ezekiel, notably in Chapter 16, God describes his relationship to his people Israel as being like that of a husband and wife. The prophet Hosea uses the same bold image. As we have read, in the New Testament Paul is happy to use exactly the same imagery for how the church and Christ are linked.

Sex then is valuable; it is created by God. It is designed into the human race and is part of our make-up. That it has become affected by our sin is tragic but it doesn't alter the fact that it is a precious gift from God.

I think three things about sex come out of this:

- First, sex is not something dirty and shabby. Some people may have made it a sordid business but that is the result of them debasing it. Christianity teaches that sex is valuable and – in its place – honourable and good.

- Secondly, because it is created by God, sex is special and is not to be indulged in casually. The negative attitude that the Bible has towards casual sex is not because it is against sex. It is because it is pro-sex that it hates the cheapening and debasing of what is so valuable.

- Thirdly, sex involves the core of our lives. Sexual relations are not simply a more intimate version of shaking hands; they involve powerful psychological and spiritual processes. Marriage is the only context for sex. Only there, between one man and one woman, protected by sworn promises of loyalty and in a setting of social, personal and emotional union, can sex blossom without causing harm.

It is because God has got such a strong and high view of marriage that he gives this commandment against adultery. Adultery destroys the marriage that exists. Another person can only come into a marriage relationship at the expense of the existing relationship. When one partner starts getting involved with someone else – and it can happen well before any physical act of sex has occurred – real damage has been done in the areas of having trust in each other and keeping promises.

The Bible is plain that God created sex. It also makes it plain that sex is only for use within marriage and not outside it. The result is that we are commanded to either have sex within marriage or to abstain from it altogether. God offers no other options.

OUR VULNERABILITY TO SEX
Precisely because it is so valuable, sex needs treating with respect. Sexual acts involve our personalities at a very deep level

and because of that sex is a very potent force. One of the many lies about sex is that it is 'just a bit of harmless fun' and it is a great deception that with sex outside marriage no one gets hurt. In fact they do. The hurts come in various ways and some are subtler than others. No one needs to talk of hurt to the teenage mother abandoned after a one-night stand; or the wife betrayed by an adulterous relationship; or the children injured by the disintegrating family.

The case of King David is actually a classic example of this. He was a moral, godly and sensible man who was respected by his people. Then he lusted for Bathsheba and everything fell to pieces; within weeks his adultery had driven him to lie, to scheme, to plot and to achieve the murder of a loyal comrade. The legacy of his acts linked with this adultery stretched on into the future and cast a shadow over the rest of his reign. David's example of a mighty man – it is less commonly a woman – toppled by sex can be multiplied endlessly. Lust has wrecked an uncountable number of careers and, as in David's case, bred uncountable other sins. Most of us could easily list a dozen names in the church and politics whose promising careers have been wrecked by sexual sin. Let me be blunt; personally I have never met anyone who has committed adultery and not lived to regret it. Adultery, even when forgiven, leaves a scar.

There are many lessons for us from this account of David's sin. One of the most important lessons for us to heed is how devastating the forces were that he let loose by lusting after Bathsheba. If this story had been omitted in the Bible and we had only learned it from some manuscript we might have found it hard to believe. David an adulterer? David, the psalm-writer, the wise ruler, involved in a murderous cover-up? Surely not! Yet it happened.

And it still happens. 'I don't know what came over me' says someone; it was 'a sort of madness' says another. Through adultery, careers are destroyed, loving families broken up, lifelong friendships ended, children devastated. Why is this? I think at least part of the answer is that sex can easily take the place of

God in our lives. Unrestrained sexual desire is so powerful that it is capable of overriding everything else. When the hormones start pumping almost everything – including habit, morality and common sense – has to take a back seat.

Another lesson from David's case is that adultery almost inevitably unleashes other things. Having sex outside marriage is like pulling a single brick out from the base of a wall; it is all too easy to find the rest of the brickwork tumbling down on top of you. In David's case what should have been a one-night stand becomes very nasty. Bathsheba becomes pregnant and it is impossible to pass the child off as her husband's. (In case you missed it, that is the point of the Bible's reference to her having 'just completed the purification rites after having her menstrual period'. See note at start of the readings.) As king, David cannot have it be known that he is an adulterer! He decides to have Uriah recalled from the army; perhaps the child can be passed off as premature? But it gets worse; Uriah is the model of a noble soldier and, out of a sense of duty, refuses to sleep with his wife. And so he has to be removed and a scheme is hatched to have him slain in battle.

From the moment of adultery it all starts to unravel. You do not have to look far to see other adulteries that have generated lies, deception and worse.

There is something unusually potent about sexual temptation. Not convinced? Think of how much sexual material there is on the Internet, in magazines and in the cinema. No other sin attracts as much interest. Did you ever hear of a magazine dedicated to anger? A website devoted to online coveting? A film 'with graphic and explicit scenes' of Sabbath breaking? A late night television program offering 'titillating and uncensored accounts of' lying? I thought not.

Because of this it is wise for us to have a hearty respect for sexual temptation. I think it is safe to say that it has destroyed better men and women than you or I.

OUR NEED FOR VIGILANCE WITH SEX

Because we are so vulnerable to sexual temptation we need to be watchful in case we are ensnared by it. I want to outline some practical ways that we can be vigilant.

When we think about this commandment and how we are to keep it, we need to have Jesus' view of what it means not to commit adultery. As we heard, Jesus extends adultery from the physical act to the mental desire. Lustful thoughts, he says, are as bad as adulterous acts. In our world filled with images designed to promote sexual desire, many of us find this is a troubling statement. I think in fact what Jesus is prohibiting here is 'adultery in the mind' that stops short of the actual act only because there is a lack of opportunity.

Let me give an illustration. Imagine two married men, Dave and Harry, who in the course of business conferences, end up at parties. Dave gets talking to a woman who he finds sexually desirable and he makes advances towards her. He discovers that she has no objection to sleeping with him and they go to her room. The next morning he wakes up with a hangover and a guilty awareness that he has committed adultery. Harry also meets a woman, has the same desires and makes the same advances. However, as she rejects him, his plans come to nothing. The next morning Harry wakes up with a hangover but is able to console himself that he has not committed adultery. But according to Jesus' definition, Harry has no grounds for complacency; he too has been adulterous. In his case, as well as that of Dave, the marriage bond has been breached. There was adulterous intent and that, says Jesus, is sin.

Now of course the act of adultery is worse than the frustrated plan (and has more serious consequences) but the Bible teaches that the lustful, adulterous intention is still sinful. Jesus' ruling – and common sense – suggests that what is effectively adultery can take place without the physical act. Because a marriage is meant to be an exclusive union at the physical, emotional and intellectual levels it can be broken without the act of sex. Long, passionate conversations across a table with a friend at work with only the slightest brush of hands may still be cheating on your spouse.

The practical lesson of this is important. It is all too easy to imagine the physical act of extramarital sex and to draw a line in our minds around it and to say to ourselves, 'I will never go there'. Yet the Bible teaches that we need to draw that line much further out; that we need to put a far wider fence around our marriages. Besides, by the time you have got as far as the bedroom door it is probably too late.

Let me suggest some guidelines to help you keep vigilant.

Don't assume you are safe from sexual temptation

The witness of the Bible is that David was a great man of God, a man after God's heart and someone who was obedient, faithful and pious. Yet he fell – and fell badly – in this area. We are all lesser people and need to learn from this. You may think that this is a temptation that you have fought with and won; you may think that you are secure in your marriage or in your singleness. Yet this story warns us all. Paul makes the point clearly in I Corinthians 10:12: 'If you think you are standing strong, be careful, for you, too, may fall into the same sin.'

There are some positive things that you can do to help yourself. Let me make four suggestions:

- If you are married, work to strengthen your marriage. Good marriages don't just happen, they are made and are kept going by hard work. We need to remember that, to protect against adultery it is not just in the sexual area that marriages need to work. So often the start of a ruinous adultery has been marked by statements like 'Bill, you know, my husband never listens to me the way that you do' or 'Julie, my wife doesn't understand me. You do.' Strengthen your marriage; read up on it, listen to talks on the subject and work at it. Remember that the Christian marriage is meant to grow as each partner helps to perfect the other.

- Whether we are married or unmarried, we need to stay above board in all that we do. We must make sure that no ambiguity can spring up between us and a member of the other sex. Avoid compromising situations and if we are married, keep strict boundaries with members of the opposite sex. One common question is how can I tell if a friendship is beginning to wrongfully intrude into a marriage? The answer is actually simple. In any difficult situation ask yourself this question: Would my spouse approve of what I am saying or doing if he – or she – was standing here next to me? Would I do what I was doing if his or her spouse was present? If not, don't do it.

- Another way is to be accountable. One well-known international Christian author and speaker who committed adultery said that the thing that would have kept him from adultery was accountability. Are there a couple of people you can meet with on a regular basis? Perhaps every month or so, with whom you can honestly share your most personal temptations and pressures? Be accountable.

- Deepen your spiritual life. The best way to resist the temptation to infidelity is to root your life (whether you are single or married) in the rich soil of God's confirming love. Seek to know him better through prayer and the reading of his word.

Keep busy, doing what you are supposed to be doing

There is an interesting note at the start of the story of David's sin in I Samuel 11. 'The following spring, the time of year when kings go to war, King David sent Joab and the Israelite army to destroy the Ammonites. In the process they laid siege to the city of Rabbah. But David stayed behind in Jerusalem.' The writer hints that, although David's presence as Commander-in-Chief was expected in the war, he stayed behind instead. Had he been there with his troops the disastrous episode of Bathsheba might not have happened. The old rule that 'the Devil finds work for idle hands' proved true here. David was in a place where he shouldn't have been. He should have been away at the war but instead he was at home. Often temptation comes when we put ourselves in places we shouldn't be.

Don't play with sexual temptation

Presumably, David was doing no wrong being on the roof of his palace and his first glimpse of Bathsheba bathing may have been totally innocent. Where sin did creep in was that instead of turning away from it, David chose to act on his desires and asked for her name. In doing this David may even have rationalised that he was engaged in 'mere curiosity'. It is useful to remember that 'rationalised' is often another way of saying 'rational-lies'. But then he went even further and sent for her, and by then it was too late. There were a number of stages in this episode where David could have ended things before the actual act of adultery took place but he allowed himself to slip headlong.

The implications here for us today are major. Avoid even the mildest form of sexual temptation; turn from it without a backward glance. Acts of sexual sin start from thoughts of sexual sin. A man once went to talk to his minister about the problems in his marriage. Very soon it emerged that he had had sex with a woman from work. 'I don't know how it happened,' he said to the minister. 'I do,' came the reply, 'Had you ever committed the act in your mind with this woman?' The man confessed that he had. His actions had followed his thoughts.

Don't feed your sexual appetite; make a decision for purity in every area of your life. Remember; the magazines, books, films and TV programmes that we read and see *do* affect us.

Not to play with sexual temptation calls for discipline in the hidden areas of thought and intention; the parts of our life that no one sees. God calls us to purity in our thought-life because he knows that it is here that these battles are won and lost. Action follows thought.

If you are engaged in reading or watching pornography or

you let your mind dwell on lustful thoughts, stop it now. Get rid of the things that tempt you; confess your sin to someone you can trust and try to make yourself accountable to someone who can speak the truth into your life.

If sin has occurred, repent immediately; don't make it worse

It is an old saying that sins rarely come singularly. David's 'little indiscretion' turned out to have vast repercussions not only for him and her, but for many others who were caught up in its results. When we sin there is never 'only us' involved; it always affects others. One of the lies behind adultery is that it can be a one-off act – without implications or repercussions. But there is no such thing. And here the adultery was not the worst aspect of the affair with Bathsheba; worse was to come. If David had admitted stealing another man's wife and repented straight away, the subsequent lies and the death of Uriah might have been avoided.

The lesson is plain for this and other sins. Don't make matters worse; confession is better than cover-up; repentance now is better than revelations later. Another great lie of the Devil is to tell you that you are in so deep that the only way is to keep going forward. There is a way; and that way is out.

If you are involved in an adulterous or unhealthy sexual relationship then end it now. Repent and talk to someone about it and seek professional counsel.

THE VIRTUE OF FORGIVENESS

The Bible sets out the highest ideals for marriage. And all our marriages, even the best, fall short in some shape or form of that ideal. However, the heart of Christianity is that God is not simply someone who judges those who fail, he is someone who forgives those who repent and someone who gives strength to those who strive to keep his standards.

If the Bible speaks powerfully against sexual sin, it also speaks about how sexual sin can be forgiven. We need to have this balance. The non-Christian world views sexual sin as something of little account; while some in the church tend to view it as something uniquely abominable. The truth is that while it is terrible, it is not the only sin and it is not an unforgivable sin.

Jesus himself calls for the highest standards in our sexual behaviour yet always talks about forgiveness to those who have fallen short and seek help. He was known as a friend of sinners. The passage in John 8:1–11 is the classic passage on this. Here, in order to trap Jesus, a woman who has been caught in the act of adultery is brought to him. The question posed to him is whether – as the Old Testament law demanded – she should be stoned to death. Jesus' answer is surprisingly devastating; those without sin are to throw the first stone. We read that starting with the oldest they walked away. Jesus who, as the only one without sin, could have thrown a stone, doesn't. Instead, he speaks to her gently telling her he doesn't condemn her and then orders her to 'go, and sin no more'.

There is everything here; forgiveness, no condemnation, and the instruction to live a new and pure life.

There is an important point to make to those of you who have been Christians for many years. It is probably now safe to assume that if anyone older than sixteen becomes a Christian today, they will be coming into the church with a history of sexual activity and weighed down by a rucksack of hurts, habits and hang-ups. Some will have had complex and troubled relationships that will need unravelling. For those brought up in a different moral climate it is easy to be judgmental but the challenge to us in the church is, without downplaying the teaching of the Bible, to show such people wisdom, compassion and love. We need to be able to hold out acceptance, forgiveness and the call to sexual purity at the same time.

CONCLUSION

The first thing to say is that although God made men and women to enjoy friendship and relationship with each other, this need not involve sexual activity. Because of the emphasis on sex in our society it needs to be stressed that for someone to live a single life without being sexually involved with someone else is not wrong. We have made great inroads against other forms of prejudice over the last half-century but modern society comes down hard on single people. The great lie today is that if you do not have a sexual partner you must be frustrated, a failure or a freak. The harm that lie has done is beyond measure. No, we need to emphasise again and again that to be single is a valid state. That Jesus was unmarried should stop any thoughts that being single is a second-class form of living. Having said that we need to realise that this has implications for us. Churches are quick to criticise Christians who go out with non-Christians but they can be less speedy at encouraging a social life that goes out of its way to include singles.

In terms of sex we have to say that God made men and women for physical intimacy only within the lifelong, committed and faithful relationship of marriage. Sex is the sealing and celebration of that intimacy and exclusiveness. It is entirely appropriate and right within a married relationship. It is entirely inappropriate and wrong outside of that relationship.

Because of its value, sex should not be treated lightly; because of its power sex should not be treated casually. We all need to take the appropriate action to ensure that our lives honour God in this area. We live in a society where the Bible's standard is unusual and looked upon either with amazement, contempt or disbelief. Increasingly the way that Christians deal with sex will make us stand out.

7) SUGGESTED PRAYERS

PRAYER OF CONFESSION

Loving Father God, you are the God of all faithfulness and you keep your promises for ever. You are the giver of all good gifts, the provider of all our relationships and desire. We praise you for the way that you made us in your image, male and female, to share your love and bring you praise.

God our Father, we acknowledge that you are a God of holiness and purity. You have called us through Jesus Christ to be your children and, as those children, to take on your standards for our lives. We acknowledge that in this area of sexual sin we have so often fallen to the standards of the world about us; we have had wrong desires and thoughts, said wrong words and some of us have committed wrong actions. We admit the rightness of your standards and confess our faults and failings.

Forgive us dear Lord for what we have done with the gifts that you give us through each other. Restore us and make us a people of your own possession. May we honour you in all our relationships and with our bodies. May we witness to your purity and faithfulness as we celebrate the gifts of life and love that you have given. For the sake of our LORD Jesus, Amen.

PRAYER OF COMMITMENT

Lord, we come before you now and ask for your forgiveness in this area of our lives. Cleanse us, we pray, and create in us clean hearts. Give us a desire for purity in thought, word and deed. We ask that, from this day on, we might have the wisdom and grace through the power of your Holy Spirit to keep your standards in the midst of a world that has devalued your gift of sex and marriage.

Father we ask that you will protect us and our families, from error and sin in this area. Help us to serve you faithfully in whatever state of life you call us to be. May we be those who value and honour marriage and help us to support those who are passing through difficulties and temptations in this area.

Glorify your name we pray in this area of our lives through Jesus Christ our Lord, Amen.

Service Outline 5

Don't Murder!

Commandment 6: Exodus 20:13 'Do not murder.'

[Note: Dealing with this commandment presents several difficulties. In the first place, it is one commandment that most people think that they are not judged by. Few people in the average church would admit to being murderers. Secondly, while I believe this commandment does apply to abortion, this is a hard subject to preach on and one that can easily deepen the grief and guilt of those who have had an abortion. Nevertheless, abortion cannot be excluded. There are too, other practical areas of 'taking life' that we should think about. Thirdly, Jesus' expansion of this commandment into the area of anger is not without its difficulties to the modern mind. I have tried to link the two parts by talking about Deadly Actions and Deadly Emotions.]

1) SUGGESTED HYMNS AND SONG

HYMNS
- All praise to our redeeming Lord [C. Wesley]
- God of Grace and God of Glory
- Eternal Father strong to save
- O God of love, O King of peace
- God the omnipotent, King who ordainest

SONGS
- Who can sound the depths of sorrow
- Make me a channel of your peace (various versions)
- How lovely on the mountains are the feet of him

- Let me have my way among you (Do not strive)
- God will keep you in perfect peace
- Beauty for brokenness
- Show me the way of the cross [Matt Redman]
- Servant King

2) WARM-UP ACTIVITIES AND ILLUSTRATIONS

PARTICIPATORY QUESTIONS
1) Starter
Ask for a show of hands:
Who has kicked their car? (Why?)
Who has sworn at their computer? (Why?)
Who makes you angry on television? (Why?)

2) What makes you mad when you are driving? Ask for illustrations.
[Note: Try not to let people be too offensive about men in cloth caps, drivers of white vans or little old ladies. You probably have representatives of all three groups in your congregation.]

3) What other pet hates do people have?

ILLUSTRATIONS
- Violent crime is on the increase. In 1950 there were around 4000 cases of what is called 'violence against the person' in England and Wales. In 1998 for a population only a quarter larger, there were 61,000 cases. *[Note: More recent statistics may be available by the time this is published; try **www.statsbase.gov.uk**.]*
- A recent study indicates that, of Britain's some 2.8 million company car drivers, about 83% have been victims of some form of road rage during their working life. About 21% reported having been run off the road and 18% have been physically threatened by another driver.
- During the 20th century over 500 million people lost their lives due to warfare.

3) CHILDREN'S ACTIVITY

PREPARATION

You will need
- a number of pound coins
- a single penny
- a stop watch

ACTIVITY

Question: Who is fast at counting?

Imagine you had a line of pound coins. *[Note: Illustrate.]*

Question: How many could you count in a minute?

Get a volunteer to count one, two, three, etc. aloud over a timed thirty seconds. Double it. The figure you should get is about a hundred in a minute.

Question: In 1996 Alan Shearer was transferred from Blackburn Rovers to Newcastle United for how much money? Guess.

Answer: 15 million pounds.

[Note: At the time of writing, Shearer's fee was the UK record but it will probably be beaten one day. If so adjust the illustration accordingly.]

Question: That is 15 thousand thousand pound coins. If you could count them a hundred a minute and do not stop, how long would that take?

Have guesses.

Answer: 150,000 minutes. That is 2,500 hours or just over a hundred days! With no breaks for sleeping, eating or drinking.

Question: So Alan Shearer was worth 15 million pounds. What are you worth?

Pick up a penny.

Question: Not worth much is it? What can I buy with it?

[Note: Might joke about two of Alan Shearer's hairs.]

Question: If I took a hammer and smashed it I would be committing a crime. *[Note: Unlikely to go to court as the 1936 Coinage Act has been repealed and the later acts on coinage do not refer to it. But according to the Royal Mint, the Lord Chancellor's Office still 'frowns on it'. But this is a children's talk...]* Why?

Answer: I would be defacing the Queen's image. It is insulting her.

Now the Bible says that we are all like this coin. We are all made in God's image; that means we all have God's picture stamped on us.

CONCLUSION

We need to remember two things:

i) *We* are valuable. How much are you worth? An enormous amount. In fact even Alan Shearer is undervalued. God loves us so much that he died for us.

ii) *People* we meet are valuable. That is why it is wrong to hate or hurt people. To destroy a human life is to destroy something with God's name on. If you hate someone so much you want to hurt them then you are defacing God's image.

4) BIBLE READINGS

OLD TESTAMENT
Genesis 1:26–27; Genesis 9:1–6, Psalm 8:1–9

The Old Testament readings concentrate on passages that demonstrate how valuable human life is.

CAST
Introducer: As above
Text Narrator: As above
The Lord: As above
David: Needs a tone of wonder

Introducer: At the very start of the Bible God explains that there is something very special about human beings.

Text Narrator: Then God said...

The Lord: Let us make people in our image, to be like ourselves. They will be masters over all life – the fish in the sea, the birds in the sky, and all the livestock, wild animals, and small animals.

Text Narrator: So God created people in his own image; God patterned them after himself; male and female he created them.

(Genesis 1:26–27)

Introducer: From this we see that men and women are different from animals and birds. We have something in us that marks us out as being in the image of God, of having some of his characteristics. Later, after the great flood, God spoke to Noah about how he and his descendants were to live.

Text Narrator: God blessed Noah and his sons and told them,

The LORD: Multiply and fill the earth. All the wild animals, large and small, and all the birds and fish will be afraid of you. I have placed them in your power. I have given them to you for food, just as I have given you grain and vegetables. But you must never eat animals that still have their lifeblood in them. And murder is forbidden. Animals that kill people must die, and any person who murders must be killed. Yes, you must execute anyone who murders another person, for to kill a person is to kill a living being made in God's image.

(Genesis 9:1–6)

Introducer: According to this, murder is such a serious offence because human beings are made in God's image. In Psalm Eight David talks further of how valuable people are.

David:
O LORD, our LORD, the majesty of your name fills the earth!

Your glory is higher than the heavens.

You have taught children and nursing infants to give you
    praise.

They silence your enemies who were seeking revenge.

When I look at the night sky and see the work of your
    fingers –

the moon and the stars you have set in place –

what are mortals that you should think of us,

mere humans that you should care for us?

For you made us only a little lower than God,

and you crowned us with glory and honour.

You put us in charge of everything you made,

giving us authority over all things –

the sheep and the cattle and all the wild animals,

the birds in the sky, the fish in the sea,

and everything that swims the ocean currents.

O LORD, our LORD, the majesty of your name fills the
    earth!

(Psalm 8:1–9)

NEW TESTAMENT
Matthew 5:21–26; 5:38–42, Ephesians 4:25–27,
James 1:19,20

This is made up of two key readings from Jesus' teaching in The
Sermon on the Mount and two short passages from the epistles.

CAST

Introducer: As above

Text Narrator: As above

Jesus: Emphasise the repeated 'You have heard…but *I* say'
formula

Reader: Here quoting the Old Testament should have a stern
tone

Paul

James

Introducer: Jesus linked murder and anger in his teaching. He said…

Jesus: You have heard that the Law of Moses says,

Reader: Do not murder. If you commit murder, you are subject to judgment.

Jesus: But I say, if you are angry with someone, you are subject to judgment! If you call someone an idiot, you are in danger of being brought before the high council. And if you curse someone, you are in danger of the fires of hell. So if you are standing before the altar in the Temple, offering a sacrifice to God, and you suddenly remember that someone has something against you, leave your sacrifice there beside the altar. Go and be reconciled to that person. Then come and offer your sacrifice to God. Come to terms quickly with your enemy before it is too late and you are dragged into court, handed over to an officer, and thrown in jail. I assure you that you won't be free again until you have paid the last penny.

(Matthew 5:21–26)

Introducer: Jesus also taught that his followers were not to hate their enemies. He said…

Jesus: You have heard that the Law of Moses says…

Reader: If an eye is injured, injure the eye of the person who did it. If a tooth gets knocked out, knock out the tooth of the person who did it.

Jesus: But I say, don't resist an evil person! If you are slapped on the right cheek, turn the other, too. If you are ordered to court and your shirt is taken from you, give your coat, too. If a soldier demands that you carry his gear for a mile, carry it two miles. Give to those who ask, and don't turn away from those who want to borrow. You have heard that the Law of Moses says...

Reader: Love your neighbour 'and hate your enemy'. *[Note: The 'hate your enemy clause' is not actually a quote from the Old Testament was something that was popularly added on.]*

Jesus: But I say, love your enemies! Pray for those who persecute you! In that way, you will be acting as true children of your Father in heaven. For he gives his sunlight to both the evil and the good, and he sends rain on the just and on the unjust, too. If you love only those who love you, what good is that? Even corrupt tax collectors do that much. If you are kind only to your friends, how are you different from anyone else? Even pagans do that. But you are to be perfect, even as your Father in heaven is perfect.

(Matthew 5:38–42)

Introducer: In his letter to the Ephesian church Paul speaks about anger and its dangers.

Paul: So put away all falsehood and 'tell your neighbour the truth' because we belong to each other. And 'don't sin by letting anger gain control over you'. Don't let the sun go down while you are still angry, for anger gives a mighty foothold to the Devil.

(Ephesians 4:25–27)

Introducer: And Jesus' brother James also teaches us about how we should react when we feel like getting angry.

James: My dear brothers and sisters, be quick to listen, slow to speak, and slow to get angry. Your anger can never make things right in God's sight.

(James 1:19, 20)

5) POEM BY STEWART HENDERSON

First the treaty,
then the war
with perches
for the vulture's claw.

Legislation
put in place
thus producing
funeral lace.

Duplicitous
peak time charms,
kissing babies
selling arms.

Passion, rage,
the fatal blow.
Hidden Semtex
quid pro quo.

And where to now
with your schemes?
Seditious visions
shameless dreams.

You burn the skies
though I'm still here,
and you ignore
what should be clear.

Do not murder
do not sin.
Suspend hostilities
within.

DEADLY ACTIONS
AND DEADLY EMOTIONS

Commandment 6: Exodus 20:13 'Do not murder.'

INTRODUCTION

Two questions come to mind when we look at this commandment.

The first is this; what does it really mean? After all, didn't the older Bible versions say 'you shall not kill'?

The second is this; is it relevant? After all we have a good idea what murder is and, for most of us, it is not one of the great temptations of life. Oh, once in a while we might think how convenient it would if rich Uncle Bert died or if the boss didn't come back from his holidays, but murder? Hardly. Not us. Most of us will spend our entire lives coming no nearer to a murder than watching *Inspector Morse* or shaking our heads over some newspaper headline. There are around 750–1000 homicides in the UK a year compared to 4000–5000 road traffic deaths.

Yet when we turn to the New Testament we find that when Jesus deals with this commandment he talks about anger as being sinful because it is the desire to kill. And that is worrying; because if Jesus is right, then this commandment is not only relevant but we have all broken it many times. While very few of us have committed murder, all of us have been angry! But before we look at Jesus' words let us turn and look first at what this commandment really meant when it was given.

Firstly, this commandment is specifically about human life. It does not prohibit the taking of animal life. That is clearly allowed. Whilst animal life is treated as valuable in the Bible, animals are never considered to be in the same unique category as humans.

Secondly, this command deals with the illegal taking of

human life. The original word in Hebrew means 'to unlawfully kill' and in the society in which these commandments were first given, killing was permissible in self-defence, in warfare and, where a serious offence had been committed, in executions. In fact, no society has a total ban on killing. Some people consider that, for some crimes, execution is appropriate. Most people will acknowledge – however regretfully – that members of the armed forces may kill in times of war and armed police officers may (in particular situations) kill in times of peace. Equally most people will acknowledge (as ancient Hebrew society did) that if you kill an armed intruder who shows every sign of wanting to murder you and your family, you are blameless.

In fact all the newer Bible versions translate the Hebrew of the Sixth Commandment as 'you shall not murder'. Yet there is a danger here. 'You shall not kill' may be too broad but 'You shall not murder' is too narrow. It suggests that the only thing in view is the brutal premeditated assault with the intention to take a life. Yet in the Old Testament you could also be guilty of shedding blood (to a lesser extent) through carelessness or even by accident. This commandment therefore includes manslaughter as well as murder. Perhaps the most accurate translation is that 'you shall not unlawfully cause another person's death'. To phrase it simply; what the Old Testament prohibits is deadly actions. And what Jesus prohibits is deadly emotions.

But before we work out what deadly actions and deadly emotions mean for us today, there is something that we have to look at first. That is the value of human life.

THE VALUE OF HUMAN LIFE
One of the great differences in belief between modern people and earlier generations is the idea of what it is to be human. The biblical view is that human beings have been created just a little below God and in his image; the modern atheistic view is that we are merely the most recent result of evolution's blind game of chance. This has enormous affects on how we value human

life and we need to be careful that we do not take on board the atheistic values that are so widespread in our world.

What exactly it means 'to be made in the image of God' is not clear. Almost certainly it refers to the way humans have reasoning powers, an awareness of right and wrong and an ability to relate personally with God. But it also means that, in some way, we reflect who God is. We are like a mirror in which God's image can be seen. Sadly the mirror is tarnished and the image is dulled. Another illustration is that as a coin bears on one face the depiction of the monarch so we all bear God's picture on us. In fact when we look in the Bible we see that humanity is made in the image of God not only because we were created like him but also because, in Jesus Christ, God became one of us. For thirty or so years God took our form and was one of us on this earth. Now in heaven Jesus is still one of us.

This idea has enormous relevance to the issue of murder. People are more than just biological organisms; they represent God. An illustration that may help is to think of an ambassador sent by some powerful king. The ambassador is more than just a man or a woman; they represent the king. To honour that ambassador is to honour the king. And to attack that ambassador is to attack the king himself.

So it is with all human beings. All men and women bear God's mark on them. By respecting them we show respect for God. By showing contempt or hatred for them we show contempt for God. Deadly actions and deadly emotions are so terrible not because they are against men and women but because they are against God.

AVOID DEADLY ACTIONS

So what does this commandment prohibit today? Plainly it prohibits the sort of bloody murder that we associate with Agatha Christie or the headlines in the tabloid papers. Thankfully, this is still a rare event in our culture.

But – of course – it goes further. Two major issues where this commandment must be born in mind are those of abortion and euthanasia. Now neither of these subjects can be dealt with adequately by making a few passing comments in a sermon on the whole area covered by this Sixth Commandment. For one thing these are complex areas. With abortion, for example, a number of issues arise. For example, when should a foetus be considered truly human? What about abortion in the case of rape? What about those contraceptives that work by preventing fertilised embryos from being implanted? There are also issues with euthanasia. For example, is a brain-dead person still alive? Is withdrawing treatment killing? These issues ought to be thought through and there is good material on the subject but they do not lend themselves to instant, sound-bite solutions. And for another thing, these are not simply academic issues to be debated; they are both intensely emotive areas where there are many people who have secret hurts and deep guilt. Those aspects are best handled by private conversation and counselling rather than public preaching. *[Note: May be appropriate here to suggest counselling resources, etc.]* A third reason for passing quickly over abortion and euthanasia is that the scope of this commandment is far wider than just these two areas.

Nevertheless the level of abortion in the United Kingdom is such that, even in passing, some comments must be made. Even if we allow that the termination of some pregnancies may, under some circumstances, be acceptable, there is no doubt that the level of abortions in this country is scandalously high. Around 500 pregnancies are terminated every day in the United Kingdom and one pregnancy in five now ends in abortion. In the vast majority of cases the only reason for the abortion is that having the baby is not desirable. In this case abortion is just 'retro-active contraception'. However you view the status of a human embryo, most of these abortions – and certainly all those involving a foetus older than a few weeks – must surely fall under the judgment of this commandment. In other words many, if not most abortions, are the 'unlawful taking of life'. There are other, far better ways of handling unwanted pregnancies than abortion. However, I say that this is not the unforgivable sin. With God there is forgiveness to those who come to him in repentance.

Euthanasia is perhaps less of a hot issue but it is one where we need to keep vigilant. There are trends in our society that need watching. For instance once you adopt a practice of failing to revive terminally ill patients what is to stop you from moving to a policy of actively 'putting to sleep' the chronically ill? Once you decide that someone must meet some standard of 'quality of life' to be kept alive, who defines what that minimum standard is? With an ageing population and an over-stretched Health Service there is going to be an ever-greater pressure to free up beds and resources by encouraging the onset of death.

What other 'deadly actions' does this commandment prohibit? There is a big debate, particularly in the United States, as to whether Christians should support capital punishment for crimes of murder. On the one side are those who say that the only way to show how much we value the life of the victim is to take the life of the murderer. On the other side are those who say that executing murderers brings us down to their level.

Christians also disagree on the extent to which warfare falls into the category of 'unlawful killing'. Most agree that, when all else fails, certain kinds of warfare, for certain limited purposes and conducted in certain ways, are permissible. So, for example, an armed intervention to release hostages who are about to be shot is generally held to be acceptable. On the other hand the waging of war just to conquer territory is wrong. But there are great issues here too that need to be watched. Surely it must be 'unlawful killing' to inflict large numbers of civilian casualties during a war? And what about the repercussions of war? For instance, 'Desert Storm' may have been a legitimate war, but there must be the most serious doubt whether the subsequent suffering of the Iraqi people through western sanctions has been legitimate. Surely too the use of nuclear weapons against cities would be unlawful killing?

For most of us here this is a slightly academic debate although if you are in the armed forces or police it is something you might like to think through (if you haven't already) *before* you find yourself under orders to fire at someone. These are important issues and as Christians who have a right to vote we need to do more reading, thinking and praying over what our response should be. We cannot opt out of society.

But, of course, there are more deadly actions than just using bombs and tanks. Economic policies can kill as well. Given the appalling suffering over much of the Developing World, can we as a nation really escape the condemnation under this commandment? I believe that in this area all Christians should be doing two things; we should be giving what we can personally towards aid for those less fortunate than ourselves and we should be making sure that those that are elected to power put things like international aid and debt relief high on the national agenda.

Such international matters would have been far from the mind of the original hearers of this commandment. Yet from verses later on in the Old Testament what does seem to have been included in it is what we could call 'killing by negligence'. The killing of other people by carelessness or inattention was wrong too. If someone fell off your flat roof and died because you had not built a wall around it then you were responsible (see Deuteronomy 22:8). While you were not held to have committed murder you were still judged guilty of causing bloodshed. This view has been passed on into our own legal system where you can be found guilty of manslaughter because of carelessness. We have a responsibility for others.

This raises challenging questions. A very practical area is that of the way in which we drive. Do we drive responsibly? Do we go too fast or drive when we are tired? There are also implications for those of us who have responsibility for other people's welfare. Of course today there is a vast amount of legislation on things like health and safety at work. Many of us have to follow it carefully for fear of legal consequences if an accident does happen. The Bible teaches however that, with or without legislation we should be careful how we live and work so that we do not cause death or injury to those about us.

We need to avoid the sins of deadly actions. Human life is precious to God; it should be precious to us. We should do all we can to avoid our actions resulting in loss of life.

Let me make two general suggestions here:

- We need to hold to the value of life. In dealing with issues of euthanasia, abortion, war and punishment we must always bear in mind that the objects of our actions are treated as being truly human. We are all God's creation made in his image and as a result we all have enormous value and dignity. We must remember that.

- We also need to hold to the value of truth. We can play a vital role by demanding that accurate language is used in these matters. Human beings have an unpleasant way of being able to disguise the most appalling realities by using some harmless formula of words. It is easier to talk about being 'pro-choice' rather than 'being in favour of abortion', about 'foetal tissue being removed' rather than 'killing a baby' and about 'letting nature take its course' rather than 'causing death'. There is a whole area of military language to disguise the brutality of killing; 'neutralisation of enemy positions', 'degradation of infrastructure', 'surgical strikes' and so on. We need to have the courage to demand that the truth be told.

AVOID DEADLY EMOTIONS

Now if that was all that the Bible said about killing we would have plenty to think about. Yet Jesus goes further. In the Sermon on the Mount Jesus uses the same rigorous logic with this commandment as he did with that on adultery. It is not enough, he says, to avoid physically killing someone. To be in a furious rage with someone is to be guilty of murder. In short – as with lust and adultery – the thought is the parent of the deed and is equally condemned. You can see how it works. Imagine two people who are having a furious row with their spouses. In their anger both reach into an open drawer. One finds a rolling pin, throws it and misses. The other finds a carving knife, throws it and manages to fatally sever their spouse's jugular vein. In the eyes of the law only one of the two is guilty of murder. But, Jesus teaches, according to God's perspective, both are guilty. Intentions count.

This of course raises a number of issues. Is all anger really murderous anger? After all, someone may say, didn't Jesus get angry?

The answer to these questions can only be briefly covered here. The first thing to say is that it is important to distinguish between the emotion of anger and the focus of that anger. It's what you do with anger that counts. Remember what Paul said to the Ephesians: 'And don't sin by letting anger gain control over you. Don't let the sun go down while you are still angry, for anger gives a mighty foothold to the Devil.' His point is that the problem with anger is that it can so easily control us or, if we let it persist, allow a situation in which evil can multiply.

In emphasising that what we do with the emotion of anger is critical, the Bible comes close to the distinction modern psychologists make between destructive anger and constructive anger. Destructive anger is the violent outburst where you lash out blindly and hurtfully at someone else. You know the sort of thing; 'I was so mad with him!' or 'I could have killed her!' Constructive anger is a cooler, more focused reaction where you decide to go and do something about the problem. An illustration may help; imagine you go back to your office after a holiday to find that in your absence a colleague has made a real mess of it; files are open everywhere; paper is strewn on the floor, dirty coffee cups litter the table. You are furious. Now if you express that in destructive anger, you will yell abuse at your colleague and lash out with words that burn and sting. To express that in constructive anger is to get a dustpan and brush and set to work tidying up. Now an action this is full of all sorts of difficulties; people may see you as a doormat to be walked all over. Somehow you will have to express (either by your actions, attitude or careful words) that you have chosen out of strength – not weakness – to act the way you have. Destructive anger focuses on making a person suffer; constructive anger focuses on getting a problem solved.

Sometimes to have constructive anger is actually the right response to a situation. In fact where there is a real injustice, to ignore it with a helpless shrug of the shoulders is not a virtue, it is a vice. For someone not to be angered by bullying, or corruption or child abuse is not to be Christ-like. The prophets got angry over sin, Jesus got angry over sin, and his followers have been right to get angry over sin ever since. At the end of the 18th century William Wilberforce got angry over the slave trade but his response was not to attack the slave owners, it was to work to have the whole slave trade made illegal. That was constructive.

Jesus' own anger was constructive. Take the most famous incident, where Jesus visits the temple to find its outer courts turned into a noisy market. In Matthew 21:12–13 we read 'Jesus entered the Temple and began to drive out the merchants and their customers. He knocked over the tables of the money changers and the stalls of those selling doves. He said, "The Scriptures declare, 'My Temple will be called a place of prayer,' but you have turned it into a den of thieves!"' Jesus' focus was on cleaning up the temple and remedying the problem, not screaming hateful abuse at those who had done the act.

Yet we need to be wary even with constructive anger. Constructive anger may be the right response to a situation. But it is all too easy for constructive anger to switch into the destructive form and it would be wise to remember that *anger* is only one letter away from *danger*.

Now God (and Jesus was God) can afford to be angry because he has perfect knowledge of circumstances, he has perfect motives (his anger is unmixed with pride or prejudice) and he can express it with perfect justice. We are, of course imperfect and even constructive anger tends to spill over and cause unnecessary damage. It is a general rule that the holier you are the more you can afford to be angry. For most of us we ought to 'count to ten' (or a hundred) many times before we act or say anything in anger.

In summary, Jesus' re-emphasis of this commandment means that to wish someone dead is virtually the same as to try to kill them. Hate can be expressed by words or a weapon and can have deadly results in either case. Hate and destructive anger is wrong and we need to flee from it. Deadly emotions are as bad as deadly actions.

Now by turning the emphasis on the thought-life, Jesus broadens this commandment to parameters so wide that all of us fall under its judgement. Murderers are not slobbering brutes behind bars; they are you and I. There is a murderer in all of us.

And murder is not just a sin against a man, woman or child; it is a sin against God. When we hate a person we want to kill them; and as that person is someone made in God's image we sin against him. By hurling abuse at others we send our words against God himself. Few of us have broken this commandment by carrying out deadly actions; but no doubt all of us have broken this commandment by having deadly thoughts.

How are we to handle anger? Let me make three points.

- We shouldn't just let anger happen. So many people today just blow up; 'It is my temperament,' they say, 'I'm hot-blooded, I can't do anything about it.' In fact uncontrolled, destructive anger almost always does far more harm than good. Remember James' comment: 'My dear brothers and sisters, be quick to listen, slow to speak, and slow to get angry. Your anger can never make things right in God's sight.' (James 1:19,20.) Anger never makes things right. It's always worth reminding ourselves that exploding may destroy us as well as our intended target. As the cynical journalist Ambrose Bierce said a hundred years ago, 'Speak when you are angry and you will make the best speech you will ever regret.'

- When we feel angry we need to try to analyse our feelings. 'Counting ten' before expressing our feelings is not simply putting the pin back in the hand grenade for a few more seconds, it is to give us time to look at the situation. It may be best to step back from the confrontation, take a walk round the block, find someone else to talk over it with. For the Christian this is a good time to pray to God and ask for wisdom and grace. So instead of taking it out on someone we take it to God and talk. Analysis will help us manage anger. Ask yourself questions.
  - Is this really important? If not, forget it.
  - When I look at all the facts of the situation, is my anger justified? If not, forget it.

- If it is an important matter and your anger is justified then ask yourself how you can express your anger in a way that will make the situation better. Channelling anger positively is a great skill. One way is by a wise use of words. You might say something like this: 'You know this is bothering me. We need to do something here. How can we stop this happening again?' It is non-threatening, it is not abusive and it is trying to build bridges. It is the loving response.

There are other rules and many other resources for those people who work or live in stressful situations or who find themselves getting angry regularly. *[Note: You might suggest counselling resources or some good books; see your Christian bookshop.]*

CONCLUSION
This commandment touches on two linked areas; deadly actions and deadly emotions. The seriousness of both actions and emotions lies in the fact that all human beings are made in the image of God.

To summarise:

We must be against deadly actions; we must be in favour of life

There are far more situations than we may imagine which involve the value of a human life. It is far too easy to see human beings reduced to nothing more than a label or statistic; a 'consumer', a 'foetus', a 'casualty', an 'occupant of a hospital bed', an 'enemy' or a 'thug'. In every case we need to remember that behind the neat words are human beings who are made in the image of God. And if we revere God we ought to be concerned that we value highly those who are made in his image. Stern action may need to be taken but we must always remember people are not just biological things; they bear God's image.

But for us to keep this commandment is to be more than simply people who avoid inflicting death on people. We should be people who are in favour of life. We should be those that feed the poor, that honour and respect the elderly and the disabled, that struggle to give people in deprived areas a decent quality of life. By showing disrespect to people we show disrespect to God; by showing respect to people we show respect to God.

We must be against deadly emotions; we must be in favour of love, forgiveness and peace

Jesus' teaching is plain that this commandment can be broken in our hearts. Hateful anger, fury, a bitter temper; all are closely related to murder. When we do hateful actions, say hateful words or think hateful thoughts, it is God that we sin against.

We need to repent of our anger and resolve to watch our thought-lives and to struggle against such thoughts. When we feel anger surging through us we need to respond rightly, analysing what we feel and determining prayerfully what is the right and loving response.

The way Jesus lived, and – above all – the way Jesus died,

shows us a better way of living than by carrying out deadly actions or having deadly emotions.

Within this desire to be in favour of love, forgiveness and peace there must be a readiness to help those who have suffered through anger or violence. We need to be those who can help apply God's love and forgiveness to those who still nurse bitter thoughts and grievances and to those who now repent of deadly acts and thoughts they have committed. *[Note: May be appropriate to offer to be available for counselling for those who need it.]*

This is a hard but desperately relevant commandment in a world filled with anger and violence. Applying it in our own lives will throw us again and again upon on the mercy of God for forgiveness and the power of the Holy Spirit for strength.

7) SUGGESTED PRAYERS

PRAYER OF CONFESSION

Holy God, as we wrestle with the demands of this commandment we acknowledge that you are the one who gives life. We thank you for the gift of life to us and to others.

We acknowledge that in all human life we see, however heavily disguised, your image. Help us Lord as we look at people – especially those we are in conflict with – to see the value that you put on them.

Lord, we realise that by our actions, words and thoughts we have broken this commandment. We have hated where we should have been tolerant, we have been angry when we should have forgiven and we have been harsh when we should have been loving. We have shown unjust anger by our mouths, hands and minds and we confess that what we have claimed to be our righteous anger was less than that. As we look at the life of the Lord Jesus we see, yet again, how he set a standard of life that we have failed to reach. We see too in the hostility and hate that was directed at him something of our anger. We confess our sins of anger and hate and seek your forgiveness. Have mercy on us O Lord, through the blood of Jesus Christ our Lord, Amen.

PRAYER OF COMMITMENT

Our Heavenly Father we pray that, through your Holy Spirit, you would put in us a new heart. May we be those whose desire is love, peace and forgiveness rather than anger, hatred and bitterness. Grant, O Lord that we might overflow with your peace.

In a world of violence and greed where men, women and children are valued little more than things, help us to stand firm in the belief that all people are made in your image and have value. Help us Lord to value our neighbours, friends and even ourselves because we see you in us. Enable us Lord to stand up for those whose lives are threatened, whether by war, abortion, euthanasia or starvation. Help us to be committed to improving the lives of the many who need your help. Enable us O Lord to honour you by honouring those who bear your image.

In a world of anger and rage where people say hurtful words and think hurtful thoughts, help us to be those who turn from evil rather than perpetuate it. Grant us through your Spirit the patience to bear insult and injury. Help us to know when anger is right and when it is wrong. Help us Lord not to tolerate evil or to be apathetic about righteousness. We ask that you would give us sensitive consciences that we would be able to distinguish between good and evil. May we be those who love what is right and hate what is wrong and who, through our lives, help your kingdom to come.

Father, we thank you that the Lord Jesus came to this earth to bring life, not judgement. We thank you for the love, forgiveness and new life that you have given us through him. Help us to live our lives to bear witness to the life and the truth found in the glory of Jesus Christ our Lord, Amen.

[Note: The prayer attributed to Francis of Assisi may be helpful here.]

Lord, make me an instrument of Your peace!
Where there is hatred let me sow love;
Where there is injury, pardon;
Where there is doubt, faith;

Where there is despair, hope;
Where there is darkness, light;
Where there is sadness, joy.

O divine Master, grant that I may not so much seek
To be consoled as to console;
To be understood as to understand;
To be loved as to love.
For it is in giving that we receive;
It is in pardoning that we are pardoned;
And it is in dying that we are born to eternal life.

Commandment 5: Exodus 20:12 'Honour your father and mother. Then you will live a long, full life in the land the LORD your God will give you.'

[Note: A word of warning. The traditional family with mum, dad and 2.4 kids is now an endangered species and it is highly likely that some of those in your meeting have either come out of – or are part of – what would once have been considered unorthodox family structures. Honouring parents has a different feel to it when you aren't sure which of several men is your dad. Be sensitive; it is essential that lone parents, adopted children, children from homes where there isn't both a mother and father, all feel included in (rather than excluded from) what is going on.

There are also enormous hurts in this area. There are those that cannot forget the injuries they received in their own childhood; there are those that feel that they have failed in the task of parenting and there are those who feel frustrated because they do not see that they themselves are going to be able to have families.

Remember God is a Father, tender and sympathetic (Psalm 103:13).]

1) SUGGESTED HYMNS AND SONGS
HYMNS
- Great is your faithfulness O God my Father
- For the beauty of the earth [Horrobin-Leavers version)]
- Praise my soul, the King of heaven

- I will exalt you my God and my King [from Psalm 145; Christopher Idle, *Jubilate Hymns*]

[Note: Various other hymns to God the Father may be suitable.]

SONGS
- Abba Father
- Father God I wonder
- O Father of the fatherless [Graham Kendrick]
- Over all the earth you reign on high (Lord reign in me)
- Father I place into your hands
- Oh let the Son of God enfold you
- The Father's song [Matt Redman]

2) WARM-UP ACTIVITIES AND ILLUSTRATIONS

PARTICIPATORY QUESTIONS
1) Ask people who their heroes are. Pick on a few of the older generation and then chose some from the younger generation.

There will probably be lots of murmurs of 'Who?' It all adds to the fun! When people name a hero, ask why they chose that person.

[Note: This little survey will reveal how different the outlook and values of the generations differ.]

2) This requires preparation. What you really need is someone who is elderly, respected and well known in the church who can briefly and clearly tell a good story about how they were disobedient to their parents. The matter can be trivial or, better, of major significance. Get them to come to the front and then ask them to tell everybody about how they disobeyed their parents. Why did they disobey? What were the consequences?

[Note: The point of this is to demonstrate that family difficulties are not new. Also because the parents involved have now presumably

passed away, it allows the speakers to be honest. There will also have been a time for reflection.]

3) CHILDREN'S ACTIVITY
PREPARATION
- Two packets of sweets
- Two thick blindfolds

ACTIVITY
Ask for two teams of three volunteers. One of each team should be slightly older. One person is designated to be the 'commander', and he or she (it is subtly important not to have either two boys or two girls as commanders) should stand near the front. The second child is taken to the back, blindfolded and turned around gently so that they become slightly disoriented. The third (older) child should stand behind them to make sure that they do not fall over or hit anything. Now put the two packets of sweets up on prominent but accessible places at the front.

Using only simple orders such as left, right, forward and back, the commander on each team is to guide his or her colleague, 'the seeker', to the sweets. The third person follows close behind the 'seeker' to protect them from hurting themselves; but are not allowed to guide them. At the end of this, reward both the teams.

CONCLUSION
Discuss what made for a successful team. Why did the blindfolded child need the orders? What did he or she have to do with the orders when they heard them?

Make the point that this required successful teamwork. Someone had to give the instructions, someone had to obey them (and someone else had to make sure there were no accidents!).

God's word teaches us that children are to obey their parents. This is for the same reason; parents can – on the whole – see things much better than their children can. They are not always right but until we are old enough God wants us to obey our parents.

4) BIBLE READINGS
OLD TESTAMENT
Passages from Proverbs

CAST
Introducer
Five Readers: It is better if readers 1 and 2 are male although readers 3, 4 and 5 can be female

Introducer: The Book of Proverbs includes much wisdom on how children are to behave towards their parents.

Reader 1: Listen, my child, to what your father teaches you. Don't neglect your mother's teaching. What you learn from them will crown you with grace and clothe you with honour.

(Proverbs 1:8)

Reader 2: My children, listen to me. Listen to your father's instruction. Pay attention and grow wise, for I am giving you good guidance. Don't turn away from my teaching. For I, too, was once my father's son, tenderly loved by my mother as an only child. My father told me, 'Take my words to heart. Follow my instructions and you will live. Learn to be wise, and develop good judgment. Don't forget or turn away from my words. Don't turn your back on wisdom, for she will protect you. Love her, and she will guard you. Getting wisdom is the most important thing you can do! And whatever else you do, get good judgement. If you prize wisdom, she will exalt you. Embrace her and she will honour you. She will place a lovely wreath on your head; she will present you with a beautiful crown.'

My child, listen to me and do as I say, and you will have a long, good life. I will teach you wisdom's ways and lead you in straight paths. If you live a life guided by wisdom, you won't limp or stumble as you run. Carry out my instructions; don't forsake them. Guard them, for they will lead you to a fulfilled life.

(Proverbs 4:1–13)

Reader 3: My child, how I will rejoice if you become wise. Yes, my heart will thrill when you speak what is right and just. Don't envy sinners, but always continue to fear the LORD. For surely you have a future ahead of you; your hope will not be disappointed. My child, listen and be wise. Keep your heart on the right course. Do not carouse with drunkards and gluttons, for they are on their way to poverty. Too much sleep clothes a person with rags. Listen to your father, who gave you life, and don't despise your mother's experience when she is old. Get the truth and don't ever sell it; also get wisdom, discipline, and discernment. The father of godly children has cause for joy. What a pleasure it is to have wise children. So give your parents joy! May she who gave you birth be happy.

(Proverbs 23:15–25)

Reader 4: Children who mistreat their father or chase away their mother are a public disgrace and an embarrassment. If you stop listening to instruction, my child, you have turned your back on knowledge.

(Proverbs 19:26, 27)

Reader 5: Some people curse their father and do not thank their mother. They feel pure, but they are filthy and unwashed. They are proud beyond description and disdainful.

(Proverbs 30:11–13)

Introducer: Along with teaching on how children are to behave towards their parents, the Book of Proverbs talks about how parents are to treat their children.

Reader 1: If you refuse to discipline your children, it proves you don't love them; if you love your children, you will be prompt to discipline them.

(Proverbs 13:24)

Reader 2: Teach your children to choose the right path, and when they are older, they will remain upon it.

(Proverbs 22:6)

NEW TESTAMENT
Five New Testament Passages
These are a series of passages that talk about the issues concerned with obeying parents. They are arranged this way to draw out the goodness of families first and the potential for conflict later.

Introducer: In the New Testament the emphasis on the value of honouring parents is continued. In the time of Jesus some people had found a way round their obligation to support their parents by declaring that their money belonged to God. Such a practice brought an angry response from Jesus.

(a) Matthew 15:1–9

CAST
Text Narrator
Pharisees and teachers of the Law: Arrogant and bullying
Jesus: Should have a cool, polite, controlled, grieving anger.

Text Narrator: Some Pharisees and teachers of religious law now arrived from Jerusalem to interview Jesus.

Pharisees, etc: Why do your disciples disobey our age-old traditions? They ignore our tradition of ceremonial hand-washing before they eat.

Jesus: And why do you, by your traditions, violate the direct commandments of God? For instance, God says, 'Honour your father and mother', and 'Anyone who speaks evil of their father or mother must be put to death'. But you say, 'You don't need to honour your parents by caring for their needs if you give the money to God instead'. And so, by your own tradition, you nullify the direct commandment of God. You hypocrites! Isaiah was prophesying about you when he said,

> 'These people honour me with their lips,
> but their hearts are far away.
> Their worship is a farce,
> for they replace God's commands with their own
> man-made teachings.'

(Matthew 15:1–9)

(b) Ephesians 6:1–3

CAST
Introducer
Paul

Introducer: Paul in his letter to the Ephesians, renews the command for children to be obedient to their parents.

Paul: Children, obey your parents because you belong to the LORD, for this is the right thing to do. 'Honour your father and mother'. This is the first of the Ten Commandments that ends with a promise. And this is the promise: If you honour your father and mother, 'you will live a long life, full of blessing'.

(Ephesians 6:1–3)

(c) Matthew 10:32–39

CAST
Introducer
Jesus

Introducer: Jesus warned his disciples that they might have to choose between him and their families.

Jesus: If anyone acknowledges me publicly here on earth, I will openly acknowledge that person before my Father in heaven. But if anyone denies me here on earth, I will deny that person before my Father in heaven. Don't imagine that I came to bring peace to the earth! No, I came to bring a sword. I have come to set a man against his father, and a daughter against her mother, and a daughter-in-law against her mother-in-law. Your enemies will be right in your own household! If you love your father or mother more than you love me, you are not worthy of being mine; or if you love your son or daughter more than me, you are not worthy of being mine. If you refuse to take up your cross and follow me, you are not worthy of being mine. If you cling to your life, you will lose it; but if you give it up for me, you will find it.

(d) Mark 3:20–21; 31–35

CAST
Introducer
Text Narrator
Jesus' mother and brothers: Should have a tone of sorrow and outrage
Person in crowd: Should call out as if speaking over a crowd
Jesus: It is important that Jesus' tone here is sorrowful

Introducer: The New Testament also indicates that sometimes our duty to our family can come into conflict with our duty to God. But it also points out that when we follow Jesus the nature of our family changes.

Text Narrator: When Jesus returned to the house where he was staying, the crowds began to gather again, and soon he and his disciples couldn't even find time to eat. When his family heard what was happening, they tried to take him home with them.

Jesus' mother and brothers: He's out of his mind!

Text Narrator: Jesus' mother and brothers arrived at the house where he was teaching. They stood outside and sent word for him to come out and talk with them. There was a crowd around Jesus.

Person in crowd: Your mother and your brothers and sisters are outside, asking for you.

Text Narrator: And Jesus said...

Jesus: Who is my mother? Who are my brothers?

Text Narrator: Then he looked at those around him.

Jesus: These are my mother and brothers. Anyone who does God's will is my brother and sister and mother.

(e) 1 Timothy 5:1–8

CAST
Introducer
Paul

Introducer: The New Testament makes it plain that we are to not only look after our own family; we are to consider others in the church as part of an extended family. Paul in his first letter to Timothy gives the following instructions for the church.

Paul: Never speak harshly to an older man, but appeal to him respectfully as though he were your own father. Talk to the younger men as you would to your own brothers. Treat the older women as you would your mother, and treat the younger women with all purity as your own sisters. The church should care for any widow who has no one else to care for her. But if she has children or grandchildren, their first responsibility is to show godliness at home and repay their parents by taking care of them. This is something that pleases God very much. But a woman who is a true widow, one who is truly alone in this world, has placed her hope in God. Night and day she asks God for help and spends much time in prayer. But the widow who lives only for pleasure is spiritually dead. Give these instructions to the church so that the widows you support will not be criticized. But those who won't care for their own relatives, especially those living in the same household, have denied what we believe. Such people are worse than unbelievers.

(1 Timothy 5:1–8)

5) POEM BY STEWART HENDERSON

> This is a template
> this is an intention
> this is think outside yourself
> this is an ideal and a practice
> this is an ordeal and a privilege
> this is a discipline and enlightenment
> this is sweet seasoning
> this is bitter herbs
> this is myriad complexities

(As for you
my bruised, bewildered ones
whose parents have tainted and terrorised you –
think not of them.
Dissolve into Me, revel in Me, refuge in Me,
I Am your Father
I Am your Mother
I will give you honour
I will consider
I will rectify.)

This is delicate
this is exact
this is beneficial
this is symbolic and literal
this is priceless and ordinary
this is wearisome and heartening
this is profound
this is necessary
this will prevail.

6) SERMON

PARENTS, FAMILIES AND CHILDREN

Commandment 5: Exodus 20:12 'Honour your father and mother. Then you will live a long, full life in the land the LORD your God will give you.'

INTRODUCTION
On the surface this commandment is simple. But when we look at what it means in our society today, things become much less clear. For example, this commandment is clearly set in a culture

that has now largely vanished; how can it apply in today's fragmented and technological society? For some people the issue faced here is far more personal; they have been so badly hurt by parents and families that they cannot bear to hear anything about the matter. Other people carry a burden of guilt or regret about how they were parents. Still others feel ostracised by any talk of the family at all.

I want to suggest that this commandment applies at two levels. The first level is the area of how we literally honour parents. The second level is a broader application; it is of how we honour the whole concept of family today. In both areas we have difficulties and in both areas we desperately need the wisdom of the Bible.

Before we can look at how this commandment applies to us today we need to understand what it must have meant in the culture in which it was first given.

Families and parents in the past

In the Middle East during biblical times, the family unit formed the basis of society. Kings and kingdoms rose and fell but the family went on from generation to generation. The family of course was not just a man and a wife and a couple of children, it was much more extended, with grandparents, parents, children and other relatives all living together, sometimes under the same roof. In fact this sort of family structure still exists over much of the Middle East and the Mediterranean world. There, however educated and sophisticated a man or woman may be, a single great question hangs over any major question to do with their life; will the family approve?

Let us consider this sort of biblical family in more detail. The family was the source of mutual support. When someone was short of food or money or in trouble, it was the family that would rally round. The state did nothing except impose taxes and (hopefully) provide peace. In your old age when you could no longer work, the family gave you a guarantee of existence. The family was also the source of stability. It defined who you were in the community; it linked you to the past. That is why there are all the genealogies in the Bible. The family was also the source of security. Being part of the family also provided protection. If someone hurt you or cheated you then the family would act together to defend you. They would be honour bound to retaliate. It gave you security and a sense of protection.

So the family was important. What bound the family together were the bonds of duty, honour and obligation. From the cradle to the grave, you belonged to the family. And within this sort of family the role of the parents was supreme.

First, parents were the source of discipline. They instilled into children what was right and what was wrong. Parents laid down rules that were enforced by the family. Parents made decisions about what their children did, even to the extent of arranging their marriages. Even today across much of the Middle East it is the parents who decide for example what their children will study, even at university. This sort of discipline was, of course, important in a tough world where you were surrounded by enemies and where your fate depended on a successful harvest. The family that stuck together survived; the family that split went under. There was no room for those who went in different directions. And to enforce this discipline parents were judge, jury, and (sometimes literally) executioner. (Capital punishment by the family still occurs in the Middle East for girls suspected of sexual misbehaviour or for children who commit apostasy.)

Secondly, parents were also the source of learning. In a world with almost no technological and social change and without formal schools, it was parents that passed on to their children the abilities they needed to live. A son would expect to take up his father's trade, so learning his skills would be vital. In fact as people had to live near their work a son would start helping his father at the earliest of ages. Daughters, in turn, would learn all that they would need to know about marriage, children and homecare from their mothers.

Thirdly, parents were also the source of religious teaching.

Formal religious education was probably fairly minimal in Old Testament times. The emphasis of the Bible is that it was the responsibility of parents to pass on to their children the teachings about God, the commandments and the history of God's dealings with Israel. In a real way, the parents were God's appointed teachers. In fact, if you read the Book of Proverbs (some of which was read earlier) you see the line is often blurred between what the earthly parent is saying and what God is saying.

Fourthly, parents were the source of identity. In some ways they defined who you were. A son, in particular would be known throughout his life as the son of Aaron or Joseph. You were – and always would be – your parent's son or daughter. Even today in the rural Middle East, one of the first questions is, Where are you from? Whose family do you belong to?

Now within this sort of extended but tight-knit family, honouring parents wasn't just a good idea, it was essential. The parent–child relationship was the framework that held the whole family system together. For a son in particular, to rebel and dishonour his parents was an abomination. It was to threaten to bring the whole structure down and it was to rebel against what God had ordained.

There are two wrong attitudes that we could take towards this system. One is to be snobbish about it and say how tyrannical and primitive it is. At its worst it was (and is) oppressive; and of course it can easily be abused. Yet given the levels of crime and family breakdown within our own society, I think we are in a poor position to criticise.

On the other hand it is equally wrong to hold it up as a social model to be imitated exactly. For one thing, the exact way this sort of family system worked out depended on a largely agricultural way of life that cannot be recovered. For another, it had its share of failures. The Bible, in its blunt honesty, records example after example of what we would call today 'dysfunctional' families. So for example, if you take a close look at the story of Joseph you will see that it starts from a family feud centring on favouritism, it's about resentment and failed responsibility, rivalry, unfulfilled roles and a failure in parenting and discipline. We could equally be very negative about King David's family. David was the great leader of Israel and the model king but it has been truly said of him that although he could lead his country he wasn't able to control his own family. His children rebelled against him and caused him the greatest trouble.

What we have to do, here and in other areas, is rather than take the practices of the biblical cultures as our standards, is to find the biblical principles and apply them to our lives. But before we do that it is worth looking briefly at the situation with regard to parents and families that we find ourselves in today.

Parents and families today

In fact, albeit with some changes, this sort of traditional extended family pattern of the Bible continued in Britain until well into living memory. But now almost everywhere in the western world the role of parents and families has radically changed. Today's family has a very much looser and more fluid structure. Indeed it is now hard to define what a family is; it is easier to talk about a 'household unit'. Many people have closer links with friends than they do with other members of their family. There is little commitment to the idea of family.

Parents too have lost the status they had. Indeed there is a lot of confusion about what it means to be a parent today and how parenting is to be carried out. The whole nature of the family – and with it – our relationship to our parents, has changed so much and so fast. Some generally accepted reasons why this has happened are as follows.

- The increasing rate of cultural change has heightened the gap across generations. Think of a modern teenager whose parents are, say, twenty-five years older. At a comparable age, his or her parents did not have home computers, the Internet, videos, CDs, mountain bikes, raves, satellite TV or mobile phones. The child may feel – with some justification – that their parents lived in a setting so distant from today's world that there are no points of contact. And of course far fewer children today would even think of taking up the profession that either of their parents had. Where they do, things have changed so much that their parents cannot nowadays actually teach them much. In fact, there must be very few cases these days where parents can pass on useful job skills to their children. In many households it is the children who are teaching their parents about the computer, the Internet or the DVD. Children have always said 'Mum, Dad, you just don't understand these things'. These days they are probably right.

- The greater mobility within society has weakened family ties. Now it is normal for someone to go away to study and then get a job half way across the country; or increasingly, in another country altogether. Some parents may see their grown-up children only once a year. Of course, we may still keep communication going by phone and e-mail; but we do not meet face to face as frequently as we did.

- The high frequency of divorce in society has caused major harm to families. Many children grow up in a situation where the person who they consider 'mother' or 'father' has totally changed. And in a culture where the links between married couples are no longer considered permanent then all other family links are inevitably weakened. Families are no longer 'till death us do part' arrangements; they are temporary, loose-linked and shifting associations. The process leading up to divorce is also harmful to the status of parents. Inevitably, any abuse or contempt between the husband and wife must spill over into a child's perception of their parents. For instance, a child will find it hard to honour their mother if their father has constantly and openly treated her as a fool.

- Many functions of the family have been replaced. Education, for example, is now the duty of the state; security is the job of the police. Equally the family is no longer needed for financial support. The Health Service, insurance and pension schemes, for instance can (in theory) be relied on to provide support during retirement and illness. Equally, people in financial need are far more likely to turn to a bank than members of their family.

- The rise of individualism has had a negative effect on the family. We now see ourselves as individuals rather than as part of the family. We are our own masters, in control of our lives. We think in terms of 'I' and 'me' rather than 'us' and 'we'. We like the freedom to be on our own and the idea of a strong family goes against that.

The results are fragmented families that may only really meet for funerals or weddings.

So much for background: the question is what should we be doing about it? This commandment makes an explicit command; we are to honour our parents. And behind that is, I believe, the implicit command that we are to honour and uphold the family.

WE ARE TO HONOUR OUR PARENTS

There are four reasons why we should honour our parents.

- Firstly, here and elsewhere, the Bible commands it. Interestingly, the Bible gives no real reason for this commandment. Elsewhere though, the Bible suggests that there is a relationship between honouring parents and honouring God. For a child at least, parents stand in the place of God. Malachi 1:6: spells out the link 'The LORD Almighty says to the priests: "A son honours his father, and a servant respects his master. I am your father and master, but where are the honour and respect I deserve? You have despised my name!"' Jesus himself condemned those who used religious loopholes to avoid their duty to parents (see Matthew 15:1–9) and Paul reaffirms the duty of Christians to their parents in Ephesians 6:1–3.

- Secondly, God shows that he has a high view of parents by using the language of parenting about himself. In the Old Testament the concept that God was the father of the nation of Israel was well known (Deuteronomy 1:31, 8:5; Jeremiah 31:9). Yet it was only among Jesus' followers that the word 'Father' became used as a term of address to God. This was because of Jesus' own practice of using the word in talking of God and also his instruction to his followers to pray to God as Father. 'Pray like this', he said '"Our Father in heaven..."' (Matthew 6:9). Interestingly, Jesus also uses strongly maternal language of himself in Matthew 23:37–39 where he laments over Jerusalem. 'How often I have wanted to gather your children together as a hen protects her chicks beneath her wings, but you wouldn't let me.'

- Thirdly, Jesus personally honoured his earthly parents. In Luke 2:51 we read about how, after the young Jesus had stayed behind in the temple, he was reunited with his parents and 'he returned to Nazareth with them and was obedient to them...' While dying on the cross, Jesus arranged for his mother (presumably now a widow) to be taken care of by the disciple John (John 19:26, 27).

- Fourthly, there is a promise attached to this commandment; 'then you will live a long, full life in the land the LORD your God will give you.' God makes a promise that honouring parents is a recipe for blessing and prosperity. In Ephesians 6:3 Paul repeats this promise, modifying it for people who had little interest in the physical land of Israel; 'If you honour your father and mother, you will live a long life, full of blessing.' God views obeying parents so seriously that he doesn't just give an order that they are to be honoured; he gives an incentive as well!

The Bible is plain that we are to honour our parents. But what does that mean in practice? And are there limits?

HOW WE ARE TO HONOUR OUR PARENTS

Our relationship and responsibility to our parents varies with time and, as a result, what it means to honour them varies too. Three stages can be identified.

Obedience in our early years

The Bible is plain that, in respect of honouring parents, the main duty of young children to their parents is to obey them. Paul's ruling in Ephesians 6:1 is clear: 'Children, obey your parents because you belong to the Lord, for this is the right thing to do.'

Now this is not an unqualified rule of obedience. The Bible never expects anyone to obey any human authority when they are being asked to do something wrong. Nevertheless, the rule is plain: normally children are to obey their parents. When this period of obedience ends is hard to define. Clearly, it has ended when you marry and have set up a new family unit. Equally, when you have left home your duty to obey parents is, if not ended, now very limited.

Another part of honouring them is that of respect. We may not agree with our parents but we are expected to respect them. For someone to obey them grudgingly, muttering abuse under their breath, is not really keeping this commandment.

Interaction in our adulthood

Does the significance of this commandment completely end when we leave home or get married? The answer seems to be no, we are still to honour our parents but now in different ways.

Some suggestions as to how we are to honour our parents are as follows:

- We can honour parents by *involving them* in our lives. To exclude parents from key stages of our lives is surely to dishonour them; to invite them to graduations, weddings, baptisms and other special events is to honour them. Of course, there are limits; you don't have to invite them to every social event and the wise parent will know when to refuse. Parents can be honoured too in decision-making. To consult them when, say, faced with a career decision is honouring. This doesn't mean that you have to obey their suggestions!

- We can honour parents by *acknowledging them*. What we are is to a large extent what our parents made us and even the worst of parents will pass on some skills and gifts to their children. It is honouring them to admit our debt to them, particularly when we have achieved some honour. It is rather pathetic to hear people say at funerals 'I only realise now, when it's too late to say it to them, how much I learned from Mum or Dad.'

- We can honour parents by *loving them*. Now for some people the idea of loving their parents is a hard one to stomach. Yet the Biblical pattern of love is not primarily that of having a warm fuzzy emotion in the heart; it is of making a deliberate act of the will. To love parents is to seek their best; it is to do for them what we would like our children (assuming we have any) to do for us in turn. This could mean speaking positively about them, tolerating their idiosyncrasies and generally humouring them. Quite frequently it will mean holding our tongues and saying what is kindly rather than what you really want to say. Perhaps – and this may be hardest of all – it will mean forgiving them. Remember, God is the only parent who has not made a mistake. Here, much prayer may be needed over a long period of time.

Care in their later years

The last stage of the parent-child relationship is a strange mirror image of the first stage. Then we were dependent on them; now they are dependent on us. In childhood there is the growth of body and mind, now both are in decline. This stage can have all of the pains of raising children but with few of its joys. Yet to abandon parents in their old age is hardly to honour them. Now of course laying down rules in this area is hard but those of us with ageing parents must ask ourselves; are we keeping this commandment? Abandoning parents is no new phenomenon; remember Paul's instructions to Timothy. 'The church should care for any widow who has no one else to care for her. But if she has children or grandchildren, their first responsibility is to show godliness at home and repay their parents by taking care of them. This is something that pleases God very much.' (1 Timothy 5:3–4.)

However hard it maybe, we are to honour our parents until their last breath.

How to become parents that will be honoured

Before leaving the subject of parents and parenting there are some useful suggestions that can be made to those who have – or are about to have – children on how to become parents that deserve to be honoured.

Love your children

Work (and it is work!) at providing an atmosphere of welcome and acceptance that builds relationships with them. Give praise and encouragement whenever it is deserved. It is easy to crush and discourage children, leaving a legacy of bitterness for the future.

Be a good example

That doesn't mean being perfect, although that is to be our aim, but it does mean trying to be men and women of God. It means showing – by our priorities, by our words and actions – that God and the kingdom comes before making money, having a good time or even having a bigger house. It means admitting our mistakes but also showing that we believe in God who is a God of grace. Of course how we treat our parents is likely to be the model for how our children treat us.

Give teaching and advice

While much can be 'caught rather than taught' there is a place for teaching and advice. This is particularly true of Christian truth. Parents often fight shy of teaching Christian things, feeling that they may be indoctrinating their children. The fact is that there is no neutral ground; whatever we do and say we will communicate our values to our children. Anyway, be assured that if we do not teach and advise our children someone else will.

Be disciplined

Children do not automatically grow up to be good. Unless it is opposed, sin will fatally warp even the most gifted life. Limits have to be set, communicated, explained and then enforced in an appropriate way. In fact knowing that there are limits gives children confidence and security. Discipline itself should follow strict rules; there should never be a risk of physical or psychological harm, there should be no cruelty or rage and it should be agreed as being appropriate to the offence. And when the penalty has been exacted there should be forgiveness and the matter should be buried.

Allow freedom and responsibility

Some day our children will walk free of us; the best we can do is to prepare them for it. We need to give them as much responsibility as they can handle and to then stand by in the background to rescue them if it all goes wrong. This, of course, can be painful. But God sets the example for us again. In the parable of the prodigal (or lost) son (Luke 15:11–32) Jesus tells of a father who lets his son go, at great personal cost, fully aware that potential disaster looms. Letting go doesn't mean letting our children do anything they want, but it does mean that – as much as we might want to – we can't live our children's lives for them.

Pray for your children!

No amount of good advice or good practice is enough unless it also includes prayer. We need to pray for our children that they grow up knowing God's love and responding to it.

A CAUTION: THE LIMITS OF PARENTS

Before leaving the subject of parents, something else has to be said; it is that there are limits to our duty to our parents. The Bible makes it plain that God demands our ultimate allegiance and if our parents come between him and us then we must choose God.

Jesus' own life bore this out. In the third chapter of Mark's gospel that we read we saw how, when Jesus' family heard what was happening in his ministry, they decided that he was now out of his mind and that it was time to take him home with them. What happened when they got to Jesus was surprising. Jesus basically denied their right over him ('Who is my mother? Who are my brothers?') and instead pointed out that his real family were those who obeyed God ('Anyone who does God's will is my brother and sister and mother').

The message is plain; there are limits to the claims held over us by parents or family. In any conflict, it is our duty to God that comes first. This is an important message for those people who are in families where there is pressure on them not to become Christians or not to go and serve where they believe God is calling them.

To summarise: parents then, are to be honoured by their

children, not just in words but also in actions. That honouring, whether expressed as obedience, respect or care is to take place, not just during our youth, but also throughout all the years that they live. Ideally, there should be no divergence between what they want and what God wants. But if there is a conflict, then doing God's will must come first.

THE FAMILY AND THE CHURCH

As we have seen, the Bible is very plain that we are to honour parents. Although the Bible is less specific about families, it also seems that, by the extension of this commandment, that we are to honour the family as well. God designed human beings for a vast range of social relationships with people; and the family is the training ground in which we are to learn to deal with others. Most people who have ever related well to people have learnt their social skills in a family setting. Equally, many people who have social problems in their lives have come from families that have been – to some extent – dysfunctional. Families are vital and God is in favour of the family; the family is his idea.

Churches have a vital role in connection with families. In a world where the pressure is on the family, the church should be a place where the family is strengthened. This support might be in terms of teaching, perhaps as sermons or courses on family life. It might also be in terms of practical help; for instance there might be a couple who would like someone to babysit for them; there might be a single parent who really needs a helping hand; there might be an entire family who needs a holiday. Of course, affirming the family without making those who are not part of a traditional family feel unwelcome, is tricky.

Yet while saying that churches need to affirm the family, there is an issue here that we cannot ignore. While the relationships between parents and children are essentially the same, regardless of culture, the structure of families varies enormously. Some people claim the Bible is in support of the 'traditional' nuclear family: mum, dad and a handful of children. This is probably going too far; the Bible supports family values (monogamy, duty to parents, love to children) but does not come down in favour of a particular pattern or style of family. In fact, unlike marriage where there is a rigid guideline on what constitutes a marriage, there is in the Bible an openness about what constitutes a family. Clearly, the heart of any family should normally be a married couple; but there are no formal restrictions in Scripture on who is to be included in the definition of family.

Some Christians might find this failure of the Bible to define what constitutes a family alarming. In fact I think that it gives us considerable freedom to be innovative about how our families work. I see nothing wrong – and quite a lot right – with our family structure being stretched to accommodate all sorts of people. In a society where loneliness is a major problem the idea of other people being informally adopted into families has a lot of attraction. A family that includes parents, children, a grandparent, a 'biological' uncle and an 'adopted' aunt under one roof is probably more a family in the biblical sense than the proverbial Mum, Dad and two and a bit kids.

But if the Bible is not completely explicit about how a family is to be shaped, it states very strongly that the family is to be the pattern for the church. Those that have come into a new relationship in Christ have, as Jesus himself said, become his brothers and sisters and are now therefore part of the same spiritual family. Paul writes in his letter to the church in Galatia: 'Therefore, as we have opportunity, let us do good to all people, especially to those who belong to the family of believers.' (Galatians 6:10, NIV.)

This means that, when we gather as Christians, our meetings are to have much more of the character of a family meeting than, say, a weekly meeting of some society. All Christians share so close a bond with each other that the only language that can be used for this is that of the family. The challenge for us is how we express this practically. There are many people today who are not part of any sort of traditional family; either because of death, divorce, family break-up or because they have been forced by work to be away from their families. For people like this, our churches should act as a replacement family. They should be a structure where people can come and find meals to eat, shoulders to cry on, friends to talk with and even homes to stay in.

The idea that our churches are to be a sort of giant extended family allows a challenging application of this commandment. Some people might feel that they can take a break from working at families; perhaps their children have left home, their parents have died and they are now free to enjoy themselves. Other single people may feel that they are not part of a family. Yet, within the larger family that is the church, all of us have roles to play.

CONCLUSION

This commandment tells us that God wants us to honour our parents. This means honouring them while they live rather than giving them a fine tombstone after they died. How we are to honour them varies according to the stage of life we – and they – are at. For those of us with children it also means that we are to work at being the sort of parents that our children will find they want to honour. By implication this commandment also suggests that we are to honour the family. The church itself is both to support the 'biological family' as well as to act as a sort of extended family.

Keeping the demands of this commandment is hard. Both relating to parents and being a parent is far from easy. Yet the Gospel is good news not bad and Jesus promised that his yoke was an easy burden not a hard one.

If you are struggling with parents; remember that God is for you. You might think that nobody understands, but be assured God does. Not only does he give you the command to honour your parents but he also gives you the power to do so through the Holy Spirit. With that responsibility to honour your parents there also comes a promise of blessing. Equally with God there is forgiveness and grace for those who fail.

If you are struggling with parenting, once again remember that God knows and understands from the inside. God is the one who calls us to be parents and the one who knows what parenting is truly all about. He wants us to be those who make the family work. He loves our children more than we do and wants to see them grow up to be godly men and women.

It you are struggling with trying to make a family, be encouraged. God wants to help you. You may have been brought up within a family in which there was almost nothing that you feel you want to copy. Yet I believe that, with God's help, it is possible for even people who have come out of the most difficult backgrounds to create working, loving and successful families. Ask God for his help.

If we are involved in churches then we must realise that it is meant to be far more than a social gathering; it is meant to be a family. In a time when the family is in decline God wants us in the church to build tight-knit and genuine communities where people care for each other. As God has brought us into his family so we are to live out what that means in the context of the church.

7) SUGGESTED PRAYERS
PRAYER OF CONFESSION

Holy God, we praise you for the way that you have made us to be social beings and to relate with other people. We thank you that for the way that, when we open ourselves up to others, we are echoing the fellowship that exists between you, Father, Son and Holy Spirit. We praise you for the way that you designed families as places of love and support in which children can grow up to maturity. We confess that, far too often in our experience, our families have fallen short of the standard that you desire. We admit our own involvement in such failings, and come before you now in repentance, praying that in future we would be better members of the human families into which you have called us. We particularly acknowledge a failure to honour our parents by obeying, respecting and loving them.

We are conscious too, Lord, of the enormous hurts that have been created by the failure of families and we bring them to you. We particularly commit to you those of us who have suffered deeply in this area and who still bear the wounds. We ask that you would bring us healing. Where there needs to be forgiveness for the past, help us to forgive and where there needs to be a forgetting of the past help us to forget. Show us too Lord where, in our families, there are ways that we can make restitution or bring healing.

We confess our failings Lord, as parents, children, brothers and sisters and acknowledge the need of your forgiving grace. For we ask this in the name of Jesus Christ our Lord, Amen.

PRAYER OF COMMITMENT

Lord God, we thank you for the way that Jesus Christ showed the perfect fulfilment of this commandment to honour parents in the way he related to his heavenly Father. We thank you for the way that he always did your will on earth and how he honoured your name throughout his life and in his death on the cross. Help us Lord to live lives that are increasingly like his.

Our God, we thank you for the extraordinary privilege of salvation. We praise you for the way that, when we were your rebels and enemies, you called us into your family. We thank you that, through Jesus Christ, we now have the privilege of being your sons and daughters. We pray that in our lives we would reflect the fact that we are now your children. As you have commanded us to honour our earthly parents, we pray that you will enable us to honour you as our heavenly Father by faith and obedience.

Lord God we thank you that we can now call you Father. We praise you for the privileges of access to you that only children can have. As we commit to you our past failings in the area of families we commend to you our future hopes. Give us Lord a godly concern to work at producing families that better reflect your love to us. Help us, through the power of your Holy Spirit, to be those who bring grace into the lives of those who are close to us.

Help us to be committed to creating fellowships and churches that reflect your loving parenting of us. Show us as we gather together that we are brothers and sisters in Christ. Through our love for one another may this fellowship show the reality of our adoption into your family. For we ask all this in the name of Jesus Christ our Lord, Amen.

Keep the Sabbath!

Commandment 4: Exodus 20:8–11 'Remember to observe the Sabbath day by keeping it holy. Six days a week are set apart for your daily duties and regular work, but the seventh day is a day of rest dedicated to the LORD your God. On that day no one in your household may do any kind of work. This includes you, your sons and daughters, your male and female servants, your livestock, and any foreigners living among you. For in six days the LORD made the heavens, the earth, the sea, and everything in them; then he rested on the seventh day. That is why the LORD blessed the Sabbath day and set it apart as holy.

[Note: As you are aware there are a wide range of beliefs within Christianity about how valid the Old Testament Sabbath is to us. The three main positions are as follows.

- *A small number of Christians (notably the Seventh Day Adventists) worship on Saturday in the belief that the church was mistaken in switching its holy day to Sunday.*
- *Another section of the church has felt that the Christian Sunday should retain much of the character of the Old Testament Sabbath. Believers in these churches mark Sunday by strictly abstaining from all work, recreation and sport.*
- *The position of the majority of Christians – and the view taken here – is that the Sabbath is part of the Old Testament Law that is now no longer binding on Christians. On this view, the Sabbath regulations were fulfilled in Christ and have been abol-*

ished; however the Sabbath principles still remain. In other words, while we are no longer required to keep the Sabbath, it is a good thing to allow ourselves to keep a Sabbath where we rest and specifically honour God with our time.

It is well to remember that in almost any large church there will be those who hold to both the last two positions. It may be worth making plain the distinction (easier to do in print than in speech) between keeping the Sabbath and keeping a sabbath.]

1) SUGGESTED HYMNS AND SONGS
HYMNS
- Just as I am, without one plea
- Dear Lord and Father of mankind (See also the *Jubilate Hymns* version)
- Come let us with our Lord arise [Charles Wesley]
- King of glory, King of peace
- O day of rest and gladness
- All the days we will bless the Lord [Timothy Dudley-Smith]
- To thee O Lord our hearts we raise (To you O Lord, *Jubilate Hymns* version)

SONGS
- Better is one day [Matt Redman]
- As we are gathered
- Come on and celebrate
- I will enter his gates

2) WARM-UP ACTIVITIES AND ILLUSTRATIONS
PARTICIPATORY QUESTIONS
Working on Sunday

Preparations
- A Sunday paper (could be last week's to avoid hurting the opinions of some)
- A Monday paper

Questions

1) Display Sunday paper. Should I have bought it? Why not?
2) If I read the online version on the computer would that be different?
3) Bring out Monday's paper. Point out that this is printed on Sunday. Why is this okay?

Point out the difficulties involved in keeping Sunday special.

[Note: the point is not to ridicule those with strong beliefs in this area but to point out how hard the issues are.]

The changing face of Sunday: Interview

Preparations

- Need to have briefed someone elderly in the congregation who has been resident in the area for years.

Interview

Have a senior member of the congregation up and ask them questions

- How far back can you remember Sundays? [1940s, 50s?]
- What ways was Sunday different then?
- What shops were open?
- What did you do as a young person on Sunday?
- What was there on the television or the radio on Sunday?
- Did you look forward to Sunday or hate it?

Draw from this how things have changed.

3) CHILDREN'S ACTIVITY
PREPARATION

- Have a variety of sheets of paper of various sizes (A3, A4, etc) and thicknesses.
- The usual sweets for a reward.

ACTIVITY
- Give out a sheet of paper to the children. Keep one in your own hand.
- Explain that they are going to do a folding paper test. Normally, each day they would fold a piece of paper in half and then, the next day, in half again. Demonstrate by showing how you fold a piece of paper. Today, you say, you are going to speed it up.
- When you call out Day One! and so on they have to neatly fold the paper in half. When they can no longer fold the paper any more they should put their hand up. The winner is the one who can fold it the most times.
- Call out Day One, Day Two, etc.

[Note: Perhaps surprisingly, no one – whatever the paper – will get beyond six (or just possibly seven) folds.]

CONCLUSION
Explain that we are like a bit of paper. We are of different sizes and shapes but each day we work it is like being folded over. *[Demonstrate.]* By the time we have worked five or six days we have had enough. The only thing we can do is to take a rest and unfold. *[Demonstrate.]* That is why we need a rest on a Sunday. God made us and knows that one day in seven it is essential that we relax or take time out.

4) BIBLE READINGS
OLD TESTAMENT READINGS
Genesis 2:1–3

CAST
Introducer
Text Narrator

Introducer: At the beginning of the Bible we read how God worked six days and rested on the seventh day.

Text Narrator: So the creation of the heavens and the earth and everything in them was completed. On the seventh day, having finished his task, God rested from all his work. And God blessed the seventh day and declared it holy, because it was the day when he rested from his work of creation.

(Genesis 2:1–3)

Exodus 16:13b–30

CAST
Introducer
Text Narrator
People
Moses: Should sound leader-like!
The Lord: As before but here slightly exasperated!

Introducer: In the book of Exodus we read how God rescued his people from slavery in Egypt and led them through the wilderness. There in the desert, God miraculously provided food for them. The way he did gave them an important lesson about how they were to use their time.

Text Narrator: The next morning the desert all around the camp was wet with dew. When the dew disappeared later in the morning, thin flakes, white like frost, covered the ground. The Israelites were puzzled when they saw it.

People: What is it?

Text Narrator: Moses told them...

Moses: It is the food the Lord has given you. The Lord says that each household should gather as much as it needs. Pick up two quarts for each person.

Text Narrator: So the people of Israel went out and gathered this food – some getting more, and some getting less. By gathering two quarts for each person, everyone had just enough. Those who gathered a lot had nothing left over, and those who gathered only a little had enough. Each family had just what it needed. Then Moses told them...

Moses: Do not keep any of it overnight.

Text Narrator: But, of course, some of them didn't listen and kept some of it until morning. By then it was full of maggots and had a terrible smell. And Moses was very angry with them. The people gathered the food morning by morning, each family according to its need. And as the sun became hot, the food they had not picked up melted and disappeared. On the sixth day, there was twice as much as usual on the ground – four quarts for each person instead of two. The leaders of the people came and asked Moses,

People: Why has this happened?

Moses: The LORD has appointed tomorrow as a day of rest, a holy Sabbath to the LORD. On this day we will rest from our normal daily tasks. So bake or boil as much as you want today, and set aside what is left for tomorrow.

Text Narrator: The next morning the leftover food was wholesome and good, without maggots or odour.

Moses: This is your food for today, for today is a Sabbath to the LORD. There will be no food on the ground today. Gather the food for six days, but the seventh day is a Sabbath. There will be no food on the ground for you on that day.

Text Narrator: Some of the people went out anyway to gather food, even though it was the Sabbath day. But there was none to be found.

The LORD: How long will these people refuse to obey my commands and instructions? Do they not realize that I have given them the seventh day, the Sabbath, as a day of rest? That is why I give you twice as much food on the sixth day, so there will be enough for two days. On the Sabbath day you must stay in your places. Do not pick up food from the ground on that day.

> So the people rested on the seventh day.

(Exodus 16:13,16)

Exodus 20:8–11

CAST
Introducer
Text Narrator

Introducer: In the Ten Commandments, not only are the details of this commandment spelt out but a reason for it is given.

Text Narrator: Remember to observe the Sabbath day by keeping it holy. Six days a week are set apart for your daily duties and regular work, but the seventh day is a day of rest dedicated to the LORD your God. On that day no one in your household may do any kind of work. This includes you, your sons and daughters, your male and female servants, your livestock, and any foreigners living among you. For in six days the LORD made the heavens, the earth, the sea, and everything in them; then he rested on the seventh day. That is why the LORD blessed the Sabbath day and set it apart as holy.

(Exodus 20:8–11)

Psalm 92

CAST

Introducer
Reader: This is a long reading; whoever reads it needs to have a good voice!

Introducer: The title of this psalm makes it plain that this is a song for the Sabbath day.

Reader:

It is good to give thanks to the LORD,
to sing praises to the Most High.
It is good to proclaim your unfailing love in the morning,
your faithfulness in the evening,
accompanied by the harp and lute
and the harmony of the lyre.
You thrill me, LORD, with all you have done for me!
I sing for joy because of what you have done.
O LORD, what great miracles you do!
And how deep are your thoughts.
Only an ignorant person would not know this!
Only a fool would not understand it.
Although the wicked flourish like weeds,
and evildoers blossom with success,
there is only eternal destruction ahead of them.
But you are exalted in the heavens.
You, O LORD, continue forever.
Your enemies, LORD, will surely perish;
all evildoers will be scattered.
But you have made me as strong as a wild bull.
How refreshed I am by your power!
With my own eyes I have seen the downfall of my
        enemies;
with my own ears I have heard the defeat of my wicked
        opponents.

But the godly will flourish like palm trees
and grow strong like the cedars of Lebanon.
For they are transplanted into the LORD's own house.
They flourish in the courts of our God.
Even in old age they will still produce fruit;
they will remain vital and green.
They will declare, 'The LORD is just!
He is my rock!
There is nothing but goodness in him!'

NEW TESTAMENT READINGS
Luke 4:14–16

CAST
Introducer
Text Narrator

Introducer: We learn from Luke's gospel that it was Jesus' normal practice to attend the synagogue on the Sabbath.

Text Narrator: Then Jesus returned to Galilee, filled with the Holy Spirit's power. Soon he became well known throughout the surrounding country. He taught in their synagogues and was praised by everyone. When he came to the village of Nazareth, his boyhood home, he went as usual to the synagogue on the Sabbath and stood up to read the Scriptures.

Mark 2:23–3:6

CAST
Introducer
Text Narrator
Pharisees
Jesus: In the first story Jesus is fairly calm in his response. In the second, there should be a barely restrained anger.

Introducer: If Jesus was a conventional Jew in going to worship regularly on the Sabbath he was revolutionary in his attitude to how the Sabbath regulations were to be applied.

Text Narrator: One Sabbath day as Jesus was walking through some corn fields, his disciples began breaking off heads of wheat. The Pharisees said to Jesus...

Pharisees: They shouldn't be doing that! It's against the law to work by harvesting grain on the Sabbath!

Text Narrator: But Jesus replied...

Jesus: Haven't you ever read in the Scriptures what King David did when he and his companions were hungry? He went into the house of God (during the days when Abiathar was high priest), ate the special bread reserved for the priests alone, and then gave some to his companions. That was breaking the law, too.

Text Narrator: And Jesus said to them all...

Jesus: The Sabbath was made to benefit people, and not people to benefit the Sabbath. And I, the Son of Man, am master even of the Sabbath!

Text Narrator: Jesus went into the synagogue again and noticed a man with a deformed hand. Since it was the Sabbath, Jesus' enemies watched him closely. Would he heal the man's hand on the Sabbath? If he did, they planned to condemn him. Jesus said to the man...

Jesus: Come and stand in front of everyone.

Text Narrator: Then he turned to his critics and asked:

Jesus: Is it legal to do good deeds on the Sabbath, or is it a day for doing harm? Is this a day to save life or to destroy it?

Text Narrator: But they wouldn't answer him. He looked around at them angrily, because he was deeply disturbed by their hard hearts. Then he said to the man...

Jesus: Reach out your hand!

Text Narrator: The man reached out his hand, and it became normal again! At once the Pharisees went away and met with the supporters of Herod to discuss plans for killing Jesus.

Colossians 2:16,17 and Galatians 4:3–12

These two passages from Paul's letters can be read together.

CAST
Introducer
Paul: Very authoritative and – in the Galatians passage – having a strong note of 'holy irritation'

Introducer: When Gentiles started to become Christians, a major issue that surfaced was over which parts of the Old Testament Law these new converts should follow. Paul, in addressing Christians in Colossae, gives the following instructions.

Paul: So don't let anyone condemn you for what you eat or drink, or for not celebrating certain holy days or new-moon ceremonies or Sabbaths. For these rules were only shadows of the real thing, Christ himself.
(Colossians 2:16,17)

Introducer: In Galatia very zealous Jewish Christians had begun to teach the believers there who had come from a Gentile background that, if they really wanted to follow Jesus, they had to obey everything written in the Jewish

Law. Paul's response to this situation in the letter to the Galatians is very strong.

Paul: And that's the way it was with us before Christ came. We were slaves to the spiritual powers of this world. But when the right time came, God sent his Son, born of a woman, subject to the law. God sent him to buy freedom for us who were slaves to the law, so that he could adopt us as his very own children. And because you Gentiles have become his children, God has sent the Spirit of his Son into your hearts, and now you can call God your dear Father. Now you are no longer a slave but God's own child. And since you are his child, everything he has belongs to you. Before you Gentiles knew God, you were slaves to so-called gods that do not even exist. And now that you have found God (or should I say, now that God has found you), why do you want to go back again and become slaves once more to the weak and useless spiritual powers of this world? You are trying to find favour with God by what you do or don't do on certain days or months or seasons or years. I fear for you. I am afraid that all my hard work for you was worth nothing. Dear brothers and sisters, I plead with you to live as I do in freedom from these things, for I have become like you Gentiles were – free from the law.

(Galatians 4:3–12)

5) POEM BY STEWART HENDERSON

Though I created you to stop,
you have forgotten how to.
And having devised your own calendar
in which everything merges –
like oceans meeting,
you are, at present, afloat
and treading water constantly.

On the surface
nothing much is different,
the waves are unremarkable.
What you believe to be the distant shoreline
is concealed by mist.
You say to yourself,
'As soon as the palm trees are in view
I will swim to the fertile coast.'

Yet below your cycling limbs,
opposing currents duel and clash,
and you have not detected this turmoil.
An undertow is carrying you
but you have not noticed.
You assume all can be controlled.

And like the shark
you will now have to keep moving,
without rest.
You have no option,
the days you have invented
demand it.
But while you are moving,
the shoreline will remain unseen.

SABBATHS AND SUNDAYS:
A LOST BLESSING?

Commandment 4: Exodus 20:8–11 'Remember to observe the Sabbath day by keeping it holy. Six days a week are set apart for your daily duties and regular work, but the seventh day is a day of rest dedicated to the LORD your God. On that day no one in your household may do any kind of work. This includes you, your sons and daughters, your male and female servants, your livestock, and any foreigners living among you. For in six days the LORD made the heavens, the earth, the sea, and everything in them; then he rested on the seventh day. That is why the LORD blessed the Sabbath day and set it apart as holy.'

INTRODUCTION

This commandment is different from the others in many ways. Most of the other commandments seem to be making a rule that was new; this commandment appears however to be endorsing a practice that already existed.

This commandment is also different from the other commandments because of the way that its application changed in the New Testament. One of the most intriguing differences between Christianity and the Jewish faith that it came from is the changing of the day of worship from a Saturday – the Jewish Sabbath – to Sunday.

In order to understand this change and what this commandment means to us today, we need to quickly look at the history of the Sabbath and what replaced it in Christianity.

The roots of the Sabbath go right back to creation. There we read in Genesis 2 that the LORD God rested from the labour of creating the world on the seventh day. The principle of a one-in-seven rest is therefore established on the first page of the

Bible. This is the basis of the idea of the Sabbath, as the Hebrew word *shabbâth* means to rest and to cease from work.

The next pointer to the importance of the Sabbath, and indeed the first mention of the term *Sabbath*, occurs when the people of Israel are in the wilderness. There, as we heard read, God so arranges the supply of the miraculous manna that none is provided on the Sabbath; but twice as much manna is given on the day before. The implication of this is that, some time before the giving of the Ten Commandments, the Israelites were already keeping the seventh day of the week as a Sabbath rest.

Actually, when we look at the Bible we see that there were other types of Sabbath. For instance, the Feast of Trumpets (Leviticus 23:23–25) was a Sabbath-rest on the first day of the seventh month, the week long Feast of Tabernacles (Leviticus 23:39) involved two special Sabbath days and the Day of Atonement (Leviticus 23:27–28) on the tenth day of the seventh month was to be an especially solemn Sabbath. And every seventh or forty-ninth year there were entire sabbath years.

But the main Sabbaths during Old Testament times were the weekly ones. Keeping them was (and still is) one of the most striking feature of the Jewish faith. The extent to which the Sabbath was kept was something of an indicator of the spiritual temperature of the times. When Israel drifted from its faith in God, the prophets frequently complained how the Sabbath was being neglected. In fact, the Old Testament prophets frequently complain about the abuse of the Sabbath and the refusal to honour the Sabbath is given as one cause for Israel being sent into exile (Jeremiah 17:19–27).

After the return from the exile in Babylon, the rigorous keeping of the Sabbath became a major feature of the Jewish faith. By the time of Jesus it was widely felt that your dedication to keeping the Sabbath was a measure of how seriously you took your faith. The result was an almost unbelievably complex maze of laws (over 1,500 rules) so that keeping the Sabbath became a 24-hour long obstacle course. Some of these regulations appear in the gospel; for example the disciples of Jesus found that to rub heads of grain in their hands during the Sabbath was considered to be reaping and threshing. There were many other Sabbath rules, some even more bizarre. Some religious experts considered, for instance, that while it was permissible to spit on a rock on the Sabbath it was not permissible to spit on dust. The reason was that by spitting on dust you were making clay and that could be seen as making bricks!

Jesus came into considerable conflict with the religious authorities of his day over the Sabbath. Although he regularly attended the synagogue on a Saturday he appears to have had little time for the regulations that had sprung up around the Sabbath. Many of his healings were on the Sabbath, a fact that aroused bitter anger.

After the resurrection Jesus' own followers seem to have started to meet together on Sunday for fellowship. Although the exact justifications for this move are not spelt out in the New Testament the underlying reasons seem plain. Jesus rose from the dead on a Sunday and his followers saw his resurrection as being so significant that to commemorate it by meeting on a Sunday would have been natural. The fact too, that the Holy Spirit was given to the church on a Sunday would also have encouraged a shift to Sunday; a day that became known as the Lord's Day. There is also the idea, spelt out in the epistles to the Hebrews and Colossians, that all that the Sabbath represented was fulfilled in Christ. Probably – although we cannot be sure – the earliest Jewish followers of Jesus continued to meet in the synagogue on Saturday and then had a separate meeting with the believers in Jesus on Sunday morning or Sunday evening.

What is very significant is that the Early Church did not simply transfer the practices of the Jewish Sabbath to Sunday. There is no indication in the New Testament that people abstained from work on that day. In fact living in the Roman Empire Christians would have found it very hard to have taken a whole day off every week. Certainly the character of Christian Sunday seems to have been different to the Jewish Sabbath. It was only later in church history that the sabbath traditions and rules were incorporated into the Christian's Sunday worship.

So how are we to treat Sunday? A widely held guideline – which is adopted here – is that while the Sabbath regulations were fulfilled in Christ and have been abolished, the Sabbath principles remain valid. In other words, while we are no longer required to keep the Sabbath in the way the Old Testament Jews did, it is a good and wise practice to keep *a* sabbath. For most of us our sabbath will be Sunday; for others who have to work on that day then their sabbath may be kept on another day instead.

What this commandment means to us today can best be summed up under five headings.

A DAY OF COMMEMORATION

A key feature of the Old Testament Sabbath is that it was a day of looking back. In fact, the first word of this commandment is 'Remember...' The Sabbath was to be a day when the people of God looked back and reminded themselves of what God had done. Interestingly, in the two records of the Ten Commandments, one in Exodus and the other in Deuteronomy, the biggest difference is found in this commandment. In Exodus 20 we read that what was to be remembered on the Sabbath was God's creation of the heavens and the earth. In contrast, in Deuteronomy 5:12–15, we read that it was the great deliverance of Israel out of Egypt in the Exodus that was to be remembered. In fact, there is no conflict. Both events are God's mighty acts; one of creating the world and the other of restoring it. The Sabbath was to commemorate both the creation and Israel's redemption.

This may be why so many of Jesus' miracles are recorded as occurring on the Sabbath. The Sabbath was the day that com-memorated creation and deliverance; what better day to restore people to health and deliver people from slavery to sin and the devil?

What does this mean for the Christian's sabbath? It means that it too, is to be a day of joyful commemoration. We too are to remember God's acts of creation and deliverance. We however are far more privileged than the Old Testament Jews; they could only look back to the creation and the Exodus. We can look back to the cross and the resurrection of Jesus as further mighty acts, which started restoring creation and delivered us from sin's power.

Our Sundays are to be days when we remember with gratitude and praise all that God has done for his people.

A DAY OF CEASING WORK

One of the great characteristics of the Jewish Sabbath was the way that all work stopped. After all, the very word sabbath means to 'cease' or to 'rest'. This was intended to be a tremendously liberating rule; on one day of every week men and women were to be liberated from the tyranny of work. Behind Jesus' anger at the way the Sabbath was treated in his day lay the recognition that this kind gift of God had been turned into a heavy burden by the religious traditions. 'The Sabbath was made to benefit people, and not people to benefit the Sabbath!' was his emphatic pronouncement. The Sabbath was to be a day of rest and God intended that his people were to be refreshed by it.

In an age where so many people are workaholics who cannot (or dare not) take a break, we would be wise to hold firmly to this sabbath principle. Our bodies and minds are made to take a regular break. To make – on a regular basis – one day of the week as one in which we stand back from what has been our work for the previous six days is vital. Exactly how that works out in practice is for each individual and each family to determine before God.

Yet there is more to the biblical concept of rest than simply the restoration of our physical bodies. There is also the idea of spiritual rest; the idea of entering into eternal salvation and security (see Hebrews 3:11 – 4:11). For the Christian, Sunday is a reminder of the fact that, through what Jesus achieved on the cross, we now have spiritual rest. We have forgiveness and an assurance of entering the promised land of heaven. If we have trusted in Jesus, we have come into God's rest. We no longer have to struggle to try to make peace with God through our good deeds; our salvation now comes freely through faith in Jesus Christ.

Linking both these ideas of physical rest and spiritual rest is the idea that we should let our sabbath day be one in which we let God bless us. It is to be a day for receiving, not just for doing. Sometimes we are not blessed because we're far too busy to allow God to bless us. Our sabbath day, whether Sunday or another day, is a day on which we should expect to receive from God. It is all too common for those that are secular workaholics from Monday to Saturday to become spiritual workaholics on Sunday.

We need to rest, in every sense of the word, in order to allow God to bless us.

A DAY OF CONSECRATION

The word consecration is not a common one today; it means 'to make something sacred or holy'. This is what was meant to happen on the Sabbath. The Fourth Commandment does not simply say keep the Sabbath, it says keep the Sabbath *holy* (see Exodus 16:23; 20:8). The idea behind something 'being holy' is that it is 'to be set apart'. 'The holy' is something distinguished and separated from the common and the ordinary.

Our sabbaths are not just to be holidays, they are to be holy days. To keep the sabbath was much more than not working; it was to acknowledge that the day was sacred. In fact, in ancient Israel this day was so holy that capital punishment was in order for those who broke it (Exodus 31:14). Actually, it was not just the day itself that was holy; it was that the people themselves were to be holy.

Our sabbaths should be the same; they should be a day when we remind ourselves that we are meant to be God's holy people. It should be a day when we ask ourselves, are we making efforts to be holy? Are we becoming more and more like Christ in our lives? Many vehicles are regularly taken off the road on particular days in order to check on how they are performing and to overhaul them. Our sabbaths should serve a similar function. They are days when we carefully look at ourselves to see if we are living up to our manufacturer's specification.

A DAY OF COMMITMENT

In Old Testament times there were two signs that you were one of God's covenant people; one was circumcision and the other was keeping the Sabbath. Exodus 31:12,13 says 'The Lord then gave these further instructions to Moses: "Tell the people of Israel to keep my Sabbath day, for the Sabbath is a sign of the covenant between me and you forever."' Keeping the Sabbath was the visible sign that you were one of God's covenant people. On that day it was obvious that you were a Jew. You were distinctive, not by what you did but by what you didn't do. When everybody else was frantically buying and selling and sowing and reaping you stood out apart by quietly worshipping God. Now such a commitment showed a real faith. It was, in a real sense, putting your money where your mouth was. You were saying, in effect, I am trusting God to look after me.

For the Christian, our sabbath is also a day to show commitment. We show our commitments to God in two ways.

- First, by ceasing to work we show that we trust God (and not ourselves) to supply our needs. All around us may be panicking by working every hour that they can, but we show our faith in God by doing no work.
- Secondly, we show our commitment to God by joining together publicly with his people in celebration. Now here, it is, of course, useful that as many of us as possible take the same sabbath and come together. The united worship of God's people on a Sunday is important; it is a visible public declaration of our commitment to him.

A DAY OF COMFORT AND CHALLENGE

As we have seen the Sabbath looked backwards and commemorated the great deeds of God in the past. But it also looked forward to the future; to God's permanent, eternal and unchallenged reign. It is a little like a cinema trailer for a forthcoming attraction. Now in pointing to the future, it is both a comfort and a challenge.

It is certainly a comfort. Imagine that you were an Old Testament Jew, working – as most did – on the land. You would be up at dawn, and probably work throughout the heat of the day until the sun had set. Exhausted, you would go to bed, knowing that the next day – and the day after that – would be the same. Only the Sabbath would bring you rest. The Sabbath must have been extraordinarily valued; it was something that you looked forward to enormously. In every way the Sabbath must have been a comforting foretaste of heaven. After all, in heaven every day was a Sabbath!

But the Sabbath was also a challenge because it reminded the believer that this world was not their home and that one day they would be taken to go and be in God's presence. That, of course, was a thought that might not be quite so comforting. It was a reminder that one day all they possessed in this world would be taken away from them and that God would demand an account from them of how they had lived. Thinking about what the Sabbath signified gave their lives a completely new set of priorities.

Of course both this comfort and challenge have even greater meaning for Christians. To the Christian, the Sabbath points forward to our future in Christ. In Colossians 2:16–17, Paul says this: 'So don't let anyone condemn you for what you eat or drink, or for not celebrating certain holy days or new-moon ceremonies or Sabbaths. For these rules were only shadows of the real thing, Christ himself.' What Paul is saying here is that the Old Testament's Sabbath rules point to the awesome reality of Jesus Christ. The followers of Jesus look forward not just to an eternal Sabbath, but to an eternity with him in a heaven where his rule is uninterrupted and unrestricted.

Now our Sabbaths (whether Sundays or not) should have something of this future aspect in them; they should point forward to eternity. *[Note: I have avoided the word 'eschatological'; some churches may be able to handle it.]* The Lord's Day should be a great source of hope and comfort to us. Today, we meet with Jesus invisibly and in a very imperfect and limited way. One day we will meet with him (and the whole universal church) face to face, perfectly and forever!

Equally, the principle of the sabbath challenges us over where our real interests lie. Our sabbaths should remind us that we are bound for eternity. That should give us a new perspective on the things that so easily preoccupy us today, like our projects, profits, pensions and pleasures. Heaven lies ahead of us and that prospect should affect how we live today.

Our sabbaths should be weekly reminders that, one day, eternity will lie before us and this world and all its preoccupations will be past.

CONCLUSION

It is tragic that whenever this commandment is mentioned the commonest response is often to argue over the extent to which the Old Testament rules apply. In fact, the whole idea of the sabbath conveys a range of enormous truths which we desperately need to hear today.

So often we think of the concept of the sabbath purely in negative terms; it is little more than a day in which we stop our normal activities. In fact, the truth is that the truly biblical sabbath is one that puts the rest of the week (and all our lives) into a proper perspective. If we neglect the sabbath principle, our lives will soon become chaotically and disastrously disordered. If we keep the sabbath principle, we will open up our lives to be blessed by God.

7) SUGGESTED PRAYERS
PRAYER OF CONFESSION

Holy God, we praise you that you are the God of time. We give thanks that all the months, weeks, day and hours we have had to live have come from you. As we think of this, we confess before you that we have not used your gift of time wisely. We have treated it as our right, and not as a gift from you. We have spent too much time on ourselves and not enough time either with you or in serving you. We repent of this and ask that you help us from now on to be those who are wise in our use of time.

We thank you too for your gift of the Sabbath rest and praise you for all the riches of meaning that there are in the principle of the sabbath. We acknowledge that we have abused your sabbaths; we confess that so often we have seen them as a burden and an interruption to our lives rather than as a blessing and a delight. We admit that we have been ungrateful to you for your gift. Forgive us Lord for this and for the way that we have prevented you from blessing us through your sabbaths. We also ask your forgiveness for the ways in which, through our lifestyle, we have deprived others of the right of rest and relaxation on this day.

We pray that you would help us through your Spirit's power to use our time right. Help us not to waste time but to redeem it, using time for your kingdom. We pray that we would understand fully the significance of the Sabbath. We thank you that it commemorates your acts of creation and deliverance and – most of all – your saving of us through our Lord Jesus Christ. We thank you that Jesus is both the Lord of the Sabbath and the fulfilment of the Sabbath and that those who trust in him have been granted spiritual rest and the assurance of heaven.

PRAYER OF COMMITMENT

We pray O Lord, that you would help us through the principle of the sabbath. Help us to see the sabbath positively as your day and as a day for the building up of your kingdom in our lives.

Grant us, Lord of the Sabbath, the ability to comprehend

what you have done for us in the past. Help us to be able to commemorate with joy, week by week, the way that you have both made us, and also re-made us in Christ. Help us to rejoice, not only in how you brought out your ancient people from slavery but how, through Jesus Christ, you have given us deliverance from spiritual slavery.

Help us, Lord of the Sabbath, to know weekly the pleasure of ceasing from work. We thank you for work and acknowledge the goodness of it yet we thank you for the opportunity to regularly rest our bodies and minds. Help us to rest so that we will be able to serve you and your kingdom better. Help us also to know the spiritual rest that you have provided for your people in the accomplished work of Jesus Christ.

We thank you, Lord of the Sabbath, that your day is a holy day. Help us to treat it as a day consecrated by you and set apart as your very own. We ask too that you continually remind us through it, that we are to be your holy people in all we say and do.

We praise you, Lord of the Sabbath, for the way that holding to your sabbath principle allows us to show before the world our commitment to you and your word. We pray that we will hold firm to it and, in doing so, you help us to trust you to supply all our needs through Jesus Christ.

We pray to you Lord of the Sabbath, that as this day looks backwards to your mighty acts of deliverance it also looks forwards to the coming of your glorious and eternal kingdom. We thank you for the comfort that this brings to us in the midst of our difficulties and problems. We pray too, that, in the midst of temptations and distractions we would be challenged weekly to remember that this world is passing away and that one day we will stand before you. Grant us O Lord, to live our lives rightly.

Finally, Lord, we ask that in all our use of time we will glorify your precious name through Jesus Christ, our Lord, Amen.

Don't Misuse God's Name!

Commandment 3: Exodus 20:7 'You shall not misuse the name of the LORD your God, for the LORD will not hold anyone guiltless who misuses his name.'

1) SUGGESTED HYMNS AND SONGS

HYMNS
- How sweet the name of Jesus sounds
- Yield not to temptation, for yielding is sin
- At the name of Jesus every knee shall bow (Note also a *Jubilate* version)
- My hope is built on nothing less
- Praise the name of Jesus
- All hail the power of Jesus' name (Note also a *Jubilate* version)

SONGS
- Let everything that has breath [Matt Redman]
- Jesus is the name we honour
- And we sing glory honour and power
- He that is in us is greater
- I give you all the honour
- In heavenly armour we'll enter the land
- Jesus is king and I will extol him
- Restore O Lord the honour of your name
- God forgave my sin in Jesus name

2) WARM-UP ACTIVITIES

PARTICIPATORY QUESTIONS
Preparations

- Find someone in the congregation who knew or worked closely with some famous or influential person (i.e. mayor, celebrity, ambassador, general, etc). This will work best (a) if they are humble and don't want to boast of this relationship and (b) the person that they knew should be someone known to the congregation.
- Discuss with them beforehand the answers so that you can keep it tight.

Warm up

Question: Who finds blasphemy objectionable? What do you do about it?
[Note: You may have to distinguish between blasphemy, vulgarity or obscenity. As working definitions as far as our language goes, I suggest the following:
- *Blasphemy is irreverent talk of sacred things; it offends against religious values.*
- *Vulgarity is coarse 'low' language; it offends against social and cultural values.*
- *Obscenity is indecent language; it offends almost entirely against sexual values.]*

Question: Who here commits blasphemy?
[Note: Almost certainly no one will admit to this.]
Question: So why are we studying this commandment?
[Note: You may want to leave the question hanging.]

Interview

Introduce the interviewee and get them to outline X, the famous person who they knew. Try the following questions:

- How did you know X?
- What was X like?
- Were you on first-name terms?
- Do you think it was a privilege to know X?
- Were they privileged to know you?
- Did you feel you had to be on your best behaviour because you were linked with this person? Why?

[Note: Hopefully you can draw out that because they were linked with this person they felt that anything they did wrong would reflect badly on them.]

- How could you have misused that friendship? *[Note: Getting favours, pulling rank, getting credit?]*
- Why didn't you abuse that friendship?

[Note: The aim is to remind people that we are careful not to misuse our links with a person who is famous or influential. Later on you will draw out that it is this abuse of God that this commandment is really about.]

3) CHILDREN'S ACTIVITY

PREPARATION

Get hold of as many products as you can that have on them the Royal Coat of Arms and the phrase 'By appointment to... Her Majesty Queen Elizabeth (or HRH The Duke of Edinburgh), etc.' This is called the Royal Warrant and details of it and a list of holders can be found at **www.royal.gov.uk/faq/warrant.htm**.

ACTIVITY

Either project a copy of an enlarged Royal Warrant up on an OHP or ask someone to read out what it says.

Question: What does this mean?
[Note: The answer you should try to draw out is that this product is one that has been approved by the Queen or the Duke of Edinburgh, etc.]

Question: Why do firms put this symbol on their products?

It encourages people to buy the product because it shows this is something that is good, of high quality and reliable.

Question: Suppose we made something terrible. *[Note: Ask for suggestions; you might go for bad hamburgers, deckchairs that collapse, trousers with holes in pockets, etc]* Could we put the Royal Warrant on this?

Try to get the following kind of responses. Of course not. It would be unfair. The Queen would be furious. Could be taken to court. 'My name on these things! I don't want to be associated with bad hamburgers, deckchairs that collapse, trousers with holes in pockets, etc.' It would be a misuse of her name. The Queen's name is to be used for serious purposes.

CONCLUSION

The commandment we are studying today says 'you shall not misuse the name of the LORD your God…' This is the same sort of thing. God is the king of heaven and earth and we are not to misuse his name. How can we do this?

- We misuse God's name when we swear by his name or Jesus' name.
- We misuse God's name when we use it to support something we are doing, especially when it is something wrong. 'God doesn't mind me stealing your sweets. God has told me to copy your test answer.'
- We misuse God's name when we blame him for his things that we are responsible for. 'It's God's fault that I failed my exam.'

We also misuse God's name when we say we follow Jesus and we are Christians but behave badly. We let God down.

We need to remember that God is someone very important and we should not use his name wrongly.

4) BIBLE READINGS

OLD TESTAMENT READINGS
Exodus 3:1–15; Exodus 34:5–7

CAST
Introducer
Text Narrator
Moses: Moses is successively puzzled, fearful and evasive
The LORD: See notes earlier

Introducer: A passage which helps us understand what the expression 'the Name of the LORD' means is to be found in Exodus 3.

Text Narrator: One day Moses was tending the flock of his father-in-law, Jethro, the priest of Midian, and he went deep into the wilderness near Sinai, the mountain of God. Suddenly, the angel of the LORD appeared to him as a blazing fire in a bush. Moses was amazed because the bush was engulfed in flames, but it didn't burn up. Moses said to himself,

Moses: Amazing! Why isn't that bush burning up? I must go over to see this.

Text Narrator: When the LORD saw that he had caught Moses' attention, God called to him from the bush,

The LORD: Moses! Moses!

Moses: Here I am!

The LORD: Do not come any closer, take off your sandals, for you are standing on holy ground. I am the God of your ancestors – the God of Abraham, the God of Isaac, and the God of Jacob.

Text Narrator: When Moses heard this, he hid his face in his hands because he was afraid to look at God.

The LORD: You can be sure I have seen the misery of my people in Egypt. I have heard their cries for deliverance from their harsh slave drivers. Yes, I am aware of their suffering. So I have come to rescue them from the Egyptians and lead them out of Egypt into their own good and spacious land. It is a land flowing with milk and honey – the land where the Canaanites, Hittites, Amorites, Perizzites, Hivites, and Jebusites live. The cries of the people of Israel have reached me, and I have seen how the Egyptians have oppressed them with heavy tasks. Now go, for I am sending you to Pharaoh. You will lead my people, the Israelites, out of Egypt.

Moses: But who am I to appear before Pharaoh? How can you expect me to lead the Israelites out of Egypt?

The LORD: I will be with you. And this will serve as proof that I have sent you: When you have brought the Israelites out of Egypt, you will return here to worship God at this very mountain.

Moses: But if I go to the people of Israel and tell them, 'The God of your ancestors has sent me to you,' they won't believe me. They will ask, 'Which god are you talking about? What is his name?' Then what should I tell them?

The LORD: I Am the One Who Always Is. Just tell them, 'I Am has sent me to you.' Tell them, 'The LORD, the God of your ancestors – the God of Abraham, the God of Isaac, and the God of Jacob – has sent me to you.' This will be my name forever; it has always been my name, and it will be used throughout all generations.

(Exodus 3:1–15)

Introducer: In the original Hebrew the name translated here as the word translated here as 'The LORD' was actually YAH-WEH. It was God's private and personal name. Later in Exodus, when Moses meets with God on Mount Sinai, God explains more what his name means.

Text Narrator: Then the LORD came down in a pillar of cloud and called out his own name, 'the LORD,' as Moses stood there in his presence. He passed in front of Moses and said,

The LORD: I am the LORD, I am the LORD, the merciful and gracious God. I am slow to anger and rich in unfailing love and faithfulness. I show this unfailing love to many thousands by forgiving every kind of sin and rebellion. Even so I do not leave sin unpunished, but I punish the children for the sins of their parents to the third and fourth generations.

(Exodus 34:5–7).

The Psalms

CAST
Introducer
Four Readers: Should have varied voices

Introducer: In the Psalms there are about a hundred references to God's name; in almost every case they occur in encouragements for God's people to honour and praise his holy name. Here are just a few verses taken from Psalms 8, 22, 96 and 99.

Reader 1: O LORD, our Lord, the majesty of your name fills the earth! Your glory is higher than the heavens... O LORD, our Lord, the majesty of your name fills the earth!

(Psalm 8:1, 9)

Reader 2: Then I will declare the wonder of your name to my brothers and sisters. I will praise you among all your people.

(Psalm 22:22)

Reader 3: Sing a new song to the LORD! Let the whole earth sing to the LORD! Sing to the LORD; bless his name.

(Psalm 96:1, 2)

Reader 4: The LORD is king! Let the nations tremble! He sits on his throne between the cherubim. Let the whole earth quake!

The LORD sits in majesty in Jerusalem, supreme above all the nations. Let them praise your great and awesome name.

Your name is holy!

(Psalm 99:1–3)

NEW TESTAMENT READINGS
Matthew 6:7–9

CAST
Introducer
Jesus

Introducer: Jesus felt it was vital that God's name was respected. The very first words of the model prayer that Jesus taught his disciples to say makes that plain.

Jesus: When you pray, don't babble on and on as people of other religions do. They think their prayers are answered only by repeating their words again and again. Don't be like them, because your Father knows exactly what you need even before you ask him! Pray like this:

Our Father in heaven,
may your name be honoured.

Matthew 1:20–23

CAST
Introducer
Angel: Can be male or female

Introducer: The Bible is plain that Jesus' own name is significant and that it means something.

Text Narrator: As he considered this, Joseph fell asleep, and an angel of the LORD appeared to him in a dream.

Angel: 'Joseph, son of David, do not be afraid to go ahead with your marriage to Mary. For the child within her has been conceived by the Holy Spirit. And she will have a son, and you are to name him Jesus, for he will save his people from their sins.' All of this happened to fulfill the LORD's message through his prophet:
> 'Look! The virgin will conceive a child!
> She will give birth to a son,
> and he will be called Immanuel
>> (meaning, God is with us).'

Introducer: The name Jesus is the Greek form of the Hebrew *Yeshua* which means 'the LORD saves'. The name *Jesus* points to what the child will do and the name *Immanuel* (God with us) points to who he really is.

Luke 10:16–20, Matthew 7:21–23

CAST
Introducer
Text Narrator
Jesus
Disciples/Followers: Several voices

Introducer: To use the name of Jesus is to invoke his authority and power. A large group of Jesus' followers found what this meant when they obeyed the command to go ahead of Jesus, announcing his coming:

Text Narrator: Then Jesus said to the disciples...

Jesus: Anyone who accepts your message is also accepting me. And anyone who rejects you is rejecting me. And anyone who rejects me is rejecting God who sent me.

Text Narrator: When the seventy-two disciples returned, they joyfully reported to him...

Disciples: LORD, even the demons obey us when we use your name!

Jesus: Yes, I saw Satan falling from heaven as a flash of lightning! And I have given you authority over all the power of the enemy, and you can walk among snakes and scorpions and crush them. Nothing will injure you. But don't rejoice just because evil spirits obey you; rejoice because your names are registered as citizens of heaven.

Introducer: Yet Jesus knew that his own authority could be misused. He said...

Jesus: Not all people who sound religious are really godly. They may refer to me as 'Lord,' but they still won't enter the Kingdom of Heaven. The decisive issue is whether they obey my Father in heaven. On judgement day many will tell me...

Followers: Lord, Lord, we prophesied in your name and cast out demons in your name and performed many miracles in your name.

Jesus: And I will reply, 'I never knew you. Go away; the things you did were unauthorized.'

(Matthew 7:21–23)

Acts 3:1–16

CAST
Introducer
Text Narrator
Peter

Introducer: In the book of the Acts of the Apostles a major theme is how the church grew by using the authority given to it by Jesus in its teaching and healing. A good example is found in this story in Acts 3.

Text Narrator: Peter and John went to the Temple one afternoon to take part in the three o'clock prayer service. As they approached the Temple, a man lame from birth was being carried in. Each day he was put beside the Temple gate, the one called the Beautiful Gate, so he could beg from the people going into the Temple. When he saw Peter and John about to enter, he asked them for some money. Peter and John looked at him intently, and Peter said,

Peter: Look at us!

Text Narrator: The lame man looked at them eagerly, expecting a gift. But Peter said...

Peter: I don't have any money for you. But I'll give you what I have. In the name of Jesus Christ of Nazareth, get up and walk!

Text Narrator: Then Peter took the lame man by the right hand and helped him up. And as he did, the man's feet and anklebones were healed and strengthened. He jumped up, stood on his feet, and began to walk! Then, walking, leaping, and praising God, he went into the Temple with them.

All the people saw him walking and heard him praising God. When they realized he was the lame beggar they had seen so often at the Beautiful Gate, they were absolutely astounded! They all rushed out to Solomon's Colonnade, where he was holding tightly to Peter and John. Everyone stood there in awe of the wonderful thing that had happened.

Peter saw his opportunity and addressed the crowd.

Peter: People of Israel, what is so astounding about this? And why look at us as though we had made this man walk by our own power and godliness? For it is the God of Abraham, the God of Isaac, the God of Jacob, the God of all our ancestors who has brought glory to his servant Jesus by doing this. This is the same Jesus whom you handed over and rejected before Pilate, despite Pilate's decision to release him. You rejected this holy, righteous one and instead demanded the release of a murderer. You killed the author of life, but God raised him to life. And we are witnesses of this fact! The name of Jesus has healed this man – and you know how lame he was before. Faith in Jesus' name has caused this healing before your very eyes.

Philippians 2:9–11

CAST
Introducer
Paul

Introducer: In Paul's letter to the Philippians the apostle considers how Jesus Christ gave up everything to become nothing by coming to this earth and dying on the cross. But that, he says, is not the end of the story.

Paul: Because of this, God raised Jesus up to the heights of heaven and gave him a name that is above every other name, so that at the name of Jesus every knee will bow, in heaven and on earth and under the earth, and every tongue will confess that Jesus Christ is Lord, to the glory of God the Father.

5) POEM BY STEWART HENDERSON

You say my name every day.
I am so often on your lips
through your instant expletives
and casual curses.
I am the exclamation
of your urges, and despising,
your wonder, and despair.
I am the empty hosanna for all your hours.
So, why do you say my name?
It is not as if you know me.
Some of you even gossip
about how you are intimate with me,
and claim my secret touch.
So why do you say my name?
It is not as if you know me.

As for your names,
they are finite.
Some are fashionable and romantic,
others are functional, quirky, plain.
Some of you have changed your names,
you are not comfortable with them,
you regard them with melancholy
and as never really yours anyway.
Some of you have borrowed names,
and over that I hear your unease.
Some of your names recall antecedents,
people who emigrated somewhere
and had settlements named after them –
your name now holding
a heritage of perished events.
See how much I know about your name.
There is so much in every name.
So let me tell you a little about My Name.

Unlike most of you
I did not need a ceremony
to receive My Name
for it has always been.

My Name is collapsing stars,
and my Name is the stallion's eye.
And My Name is the
first eyelash forming in the womb.
And My Name is the chase of the cheetah
and the earth's scarlet core.
And My Name is ridiculous beasts
and unorthodox flowers.
And My Name is
sweet savours
and pungent odours.
And My Name is that
which is too far ahead of you.
And My Name is rivers and gates.
And My Name has consequences
and My Name is an infinite scroll.

So, I say again,
why do you say My Name?
It is not as if you know me.

MISUSING GOD'S NAME

Commandment 3: Exodus 20:7 'You shall not misuse the name of the LORD your God, for the LORD will not hold anyone guiltless who misuses his name.'

INTRODUCTION

This commandment is like an iceberg; the vast bulk of it lies below the surface. And, like an iceberg, it can be lethal.

You see when we think of this commandment our attention is immediately drawn to the very public issue of blasphemous language, particularly swearing. Now this is a serious matter. All Christians find that the use of the name of God or Jesus as a swear word is offensive. To hear the names that we praise used this way is painful in the extreme.

We should not be embarrassed to gently point out that we find such language offensive. In matters of speech, most people realise that you cannot say anything you want. In these days of political correctness, we all have to watch what we say. No one would swear using the word Mohammed or Krishna. All we would like as Christians is to be treated with respect.

Of course, the real issue about blasphemy is not that it is offensive to us; it is that it is dangerous to those that do it. What we really want to say to people who swear using God's name is 'if you knew who God really is and how awesome and mighty he is, you wouldn't mess around with his name like that.' There is, after all a warning tagged on at the end of this commandment, 'the LORD will not hold anyone guiltless who misuses his name'.

But it is perhaps best to think of blasphemy as being only the visible surface of the iceberg. And although the bit above water can damage a ship it is the hidden mass of an iceberg that is the most dangerous. The fact is that there are far more ways of misusing God's name than simply swearing. As some of them are very serious and, as they are things that we as Christians can do, we need to think about these particularly hard.

I think that we can misuse the name of God in three ways; by having wrong ideas about him, by living as his people in the wrong way and by worshipping him in the wrong way.

MISUSING GOD'S NAME BY HAVING WRONG IDEAS ABOUT HIM

To understand this commandment and how we can misuse God's name by wrong thinking, we need to bear in mind two things.

The first thing is that in the Old Testament world God's name was a very serious matter because it was a part of God. To the people of the Old Testament someone's name was not just a string of letters or a label, it was that person; it represented that person. When they heard the name of someone who was powerful they felt it carried the authority of the one who bore the name. A name had weight and God's name had enormous weight.

Now, on the surface, this is very different to us today. Even if we treat people with respect (and that is increasingly rare) we tend to treat their names as something much less significant. To us, names are just words and they are different from the people. What's in a name?

Yet, in reality we do realise that names have weight. Imagine, for instance, that someone is hosting a loud party when the phone rings with a complaint about the noise. Their reaction to that complaint will probably very different if the caller announces that he is the local police sergeant. Equally, we are far more likely to be impressed by a letter addressed to us and personally signed by the manager of our bank than we are by some photocopied sheet addressed 'Dear account holder' and initialled by a secretary. Even today names have authority; they just have less authority than they used to.

In the Old Testament God's name carries weight. In fact,

the literal meaning of this commandment is 'You are not to use the name of Yahweh your God in an light, empty or worthless way.' The sin this is addressing is that of treating God's name as having no weight. In the Bible the only appropriate response to the name of God is reverence. This comes over in the passages in Exodus that we heard earlier. When God reveals his name to Moses from the burning bush on Mount Sinai, Moses' response is awe, fear and reverence. God's name is an extension of the awesome majesty of God and is treated as he is.

So that is the first thing; to treat God's name lightly is wrong and dangerous because he is so awesome.

But the second important thing about these Old Testament passages is that God's name conveys more than just majesty; it also reveals something of God's care and love towards his people. Now to understand this it is necessary to comprehend something that is largely obscured by our English translations. In the first passage that we read in Exodus, in most English versions we read that God gives his name as being the LORD, which is written in small capitals. This is an attempt to translate the Hebrew word which is simply the letters YHWH. In Hebrew (as with related languages such as Arabic) the consonants are normally only written down and the reader fills in the gaps of the vowels. But in the case of this word we have no accurate record of what originally filled in the gaps between those four letters so we do not know exactly what it sounded like. The reason why the ancient scribes never ever spelt out what the word actually sounded like was that by the time it came to writing down the Old Testament with vowels they considered the name of God too awesome to actually spell it out. When they read it aloud they replaced YHWH by a word which meant 'the Lord', a tradition taken over into English. Earlier English scholars considered that this mysterious word might have been pronounced *Jehovah* but the modern view is that the name was *Yahweh*. In fact, what it sounded like is not really important to us; what is important is that this word was not just a title like 'Almighty' or

'Majesty' or 'your Lordship', it was – in a real way – God's personal name.

This is why it is so important in these encounters with Moses; God does not simply shout at him and say 'Here I am, I am GOD!' He is saying 'Here I am; I am God but the name that you can know me by is Yahweh'. God is graciously saying to Moses, 'I will allow you and your people to know me well enough that you can use my name'. This name, the LORD, is in fact the covenant name that is used on all dealings with his people Israel in the Old Testament. To know that name was a tremendous privilege. It was as if everybody else in the world could only address God as 'Sir' or 'Your Majesty' but his people were on first-name terms with him.

As an aside for Christians is the comment that there is another reason why knowing the sound of God's name in the Old Testament is not now really important. We have a new and even richer revelation; through Jesus, the LORD can now be known as Father. In fact, for us the names 'Father' and 'Jesus' fulfil everything that the Old Testament covenant name Yahweh stood for.

So what we see behind this commandment is two truths that seem in contrast to each other. On the one hand, God is awesome and mighty and his name is therefore to be treated with the greatest honour and respect. On the other hand, God's name reveals that he cares and loves his people and that he wants to commit himself to them.

These two points help us understand what this commandment meant and what it means for us. For an Old Testament Jew to use the name of Yahweh properly was to hold both of these truths together. God was awesome but God was accessible; when they thought about God they were to think of him with both fear and familiarity. God was overwhelmingly mighty but he was also someone whom they could relate to personally. Psalm 2:11 expresses the correct response very well, 'Serve the LORD (Yahweh) with reverent fear and rejoice with trembling.'

Now whenever we come across something that requires

two ideas to be balanced, we can be sure that human beings have exaggerated either one side or the other. We can easily misuse the Lord's name by getting this balanced view of God out of proportion when we think about him.

In our present culture perhaps the biggest danger we face is of treating God with an over-familiarity that comes close to irreverence. We live in an age when God's name now seems to carry no weight in the world and sometimes only a very little more in the church. We need to remind ourselves that God is GOD! He is not to be trivialised or brought down to our level; he is the God of the universe and he is infinitely greater than we are. Several times in the Bible it says that the fear – or reverence – of the LORD is the beginning of wisdom (Psalm 111:10, Proverbs 1:7, 9:10, 15:33). If we are not to misuse God's name then we need to understand this.

But it is all too easy in fleeing from one peril to run into another. If one danger is that of trivialising God, there is a second danger; and this is the error of making God distant and inaccessible. We mustn't forget that God revealed himself to Moses as Yahweh; the God who could be known and who was accessible. In the New Testament we see the further revelation that God is the God who has come so close to us as to become Jesus who was – and is – one of us. Some people distance God by treating him as being a remote, impersonal and unknowable God, a distant force that formed the universe. By doing that we deny that we can know him personally. They misuse his name by denying that he has revealed himself to us.

So we can misuse the name of God by having the wrong idea about him. To honour God and his name we need to seek to know who he truly is and to worship him as he truly is.

MISUSING GOD'S NAME BY LIVING THE WRONG WAY

If we can misuse the name of God by having wrong ideas about him, it is all too easy for God's people to misuse the name of God by taking wrong actions.

Think of the illustration we had earlier for the children

about the Royal Warrant; the statement that a member of the Royal Family had approved some product or supplier. As Christians, God's people, we are in a parallel position but at a much greater level; we are those people who have God's Royal Warrant on us. God has chosen us and we have accepted him; the result is that we bear his mark and carry it around with us. That is a tremendous privilege for us but with that privilege also comes the responsibility of living up to God's name.

The problem is that because as Christians we are linked to God, any bad behaviour of ours drags his name down into the dirt. As a football team can be disgraced by its followers and parents can be disgraced by their children, so God can be disgraced by us. We can dishonour him by our actions.

The problem is that for many of us our walk does not match our talk. We claim to love Jesus and his word, we claim to be children of God and to desire nothing more than the coming of his kingdom; yet our actions do not match these claims. When that happens we have misused God's name because we have brought dishonour on it. A manufacturer with a Royal Warrant would think carefully about a product in case it brought dishonour to the Queen's name. We need to be equally careful about what we do.

Let's think of some examples.

- Someone puts a Christian symbol or text on their car; it says to others 'I belong to Jesus; I am one of his followers'. But then they drive carelessly, breaking the speed limit and being generally thoughtless about other drivers and pedestrians. By doing that they dishonour God; they misuse his name.

- Some one else may say, 'Oh I believe God watches over me'. But the poor quality of their work may suggest that they only believe that God watches over them to protect them. They are not concerned about the fact that he also sees their sloppiness. They dishonour God; they misuse his name.

- Someone else may make a great thing about how as a church attender they can be trusted. Yet, when it turns out they cannot be trusted to run things, either because they are negligent or – worse – because they are totally untrustworthy, then they have dishonoured God and misused his name.

There are more subtle temptations than these. For example, after a stimulating church weekend away someone may return to work, claiming that now they are going to put Jesus first in their lives. If, within days, they are doing their best to climb up the corporate ladder with a ruthlessness that is no different from their non-Christian friends, this too is surely misusing the name of the Lord.

Someone else, faced by a difficult project or a crisis, may pray desperately for God's help. Yet when the problem is over, they are only too happy to take the credit themselves. That again is misusing the name of the Lord.

The solution to this danger – and we all face it – is to earnestly desire consistent lives of total integrity; where we are righteous in word and deed. This means a life where what we claim to be, and what we are, are not vastly different.

This requires three things:

- There must be a genuine hunger for righteousness. We must earnestly repent of our low standards and desire with all our hearts to live better lives.
- There must be a total honesty. We need to continually assess how we are living at home and at work in the light of God's word and under the guidance of his Holy Spirit. Frankly, even that may not be enough. We may need to acquire faithful, godly and honest friends and give them the right to come to us when they feel that our lives are

falling short of total integrity. It is not so much 'what would Jesus do?' as 'would Jesus have done that?' The constant question we must ask ourselves is this; is what I'm doing consistent with being a follower and imitator of Jesus Christ?

- There must be persistent hard work. Whether we like it or not, as Christians we bear God's name, all day, every day. We have to live up to that not just on Sundays but also first thing at work on Monday, on Saturday at a football match and all the rest of the time too. We can never say 'I'm off duty as a Christian'.

The only way for us not to misuse God's name is to live like Jesus Christ. We will (of course) fail and have to come back to God in repentance but that is the only way to try to live.

MISUSING GOD'S NAME BY WORSHIPPING HIM IN THE WRONG WAY

Most of us talk most openly about God in our public worship. There, along with others, we praise God, sing, loudly, words about how great and wonderful he is and say 'Amen' to prayers on various matters. Yet we do not often think hard enough about how we do this.

In the Old Testament an enormous amount of care was taken over the way that the people of Israel were to worship. It had to be in the right way, at the right times and to involve the right people. The reasons behind this were plain; as one who was holy, God had to be worshipped in the right way. One fascinating feature of the Old Testament is that, in all its pages, there is no instance (as there are in other religions) of anyone trying to manipulate Yahweh. There are no incantations designed to twist his arm, there are no spells given to bind him under human control. In the Bible, God is God Almighty, far above us and he needs treating with respect. This is a truth that we always need reminding of.

Now, Christians believe that much of the Old Testament

ritual and ceremony pointed to Jesus Christ and was fulfilled by him. All rules about priests and sacrifices now belong to the past. Yet we may not have been very wise in totally overlooking the seriousness that the Old Testament Jews applied to worshipping God. Because worship involved God and God's name was a serious business.

Now, we all stand judged by this. For example, do we really give God all our attention? Are we present in body but absent in mind? Our bodies may be on the seats of our church but where are our minds? Out on the golf course or browsing the shopping arcades? God sees and he is not fooled.

When we sing hymns or say prayers do we mean them? Or are we on automatic pilot? We all have slips of concentration but do our hearts really mean what our lips say? It would be a fascinating exercise to have a service, in which a number of typical hymns and songs were sung and ordinary prayers were said and then, as people left the service, they were given a handout of what they had said, sung or prayed. And at the bottom of the sheets would be a little clause saying, 'I, the undersigned, agree heartily to all the above statements and expect God to hold me to them.'

Would you sign it? Really? When it said 'Here I am wholly available; as for me I will serve the Lord'? 'Take my silver and gold, not a mite would I withhold?' or 'You are everything to me'? [Note: You may want to add words from hymns or prayers commonly used in your own church.]

You see by singing words or saying 'Amen' to a prayer, we are agreeing with the statements expressed in them. Translated into modern English 'Amen' means 'I vote for that!', 'I commit myself to that' or 'Count me in on that'.

There is a tremendous danger that we create a culture of unreality in our churches by the way that we separate worship from the real world. But to do that is to deny that God is a reality; that he is the almighty and ever-living God of the universe. It is to misuse his name.

We can also misuse the name of God in our worship when

we use him to endorse ideas or enterprises that are not his. The most catastrophic examples of this in church history have been when God has been invoked in favour of wars, the worst of which were the Crusades. Nevertheless we have had many other wars since then that have been labelled as 'righteous struggles' or 'our Christian duty'. The historians have revealed that far too many of these have been really all about land, oil or national pride.

But there are many smaller scale examples. There are those people that have declared that it was the will of God for some action or project to be taken by the church. In fact, it was really a personal whim of the leader, the church treasurer or the building committee. Those who make such claims may have been misled by their own emotions or (far worse) they may have deliberately manipulated people by putting God's signature of approval to their own schemes. Either way this commandment has been broken; the name of God has been misused.

There are other cases where God has blessed a church or a Christian organisation in some way and those in charge have managed (perhaps unconsciously) to take the credit.

We must be very careful that we do not misuse the name of God by worshipping him in the wrong way.

CONCLUSION

Do we misuse the name of God by having wrong ideas about him? Are we too familiar with him? Do we always treat him as a buddy and never as Lord? Have we watered God down and trivialised him? Or are we those that have lost sight of the fact that he is a God who can be known personally? We need to have the perspective of the Bible that the God who is awesome and mighty is also Father, saviour and friend to his people.

Do we misuse the name of God by living the wrong way? Is there a gulf between what we proclaim and what we practice? Are we the sort of people whose lives bring credit to the gospel? We need to be those who are careful to live according to God's Word in the power of his Spirit.

Do we misuse the name of God by worshipping him in the wrong way? Do we fail to bring him honour in the way we worship? Is our devotion cold, half-hearted or superficial? We need to be people who are careful to worship God with all that we are and all that we have.

7) SUGGESTED PRAYERS

PRAYER OF CONFESSION

Lord God, we acknowledge that our thinking about you has often been inadequate and that in this area we have misused your name. We have failed to reverence you as Almighty God. Either through carelessness or deliberate sin we have undervalued your awesome power and your perfect holiness. We confess that we have trivialised you and brought you down to our level. Grant us Lord as much a vision of your might and perfection as we can bear. We would also confess that we have failed to fully appreciate the fact that you are a covenant God who has chosen to reveal himself to his people and who desires to be known personally. We pray that we would come to terms with your revelation to Israel as Yahweh and your final and complete revelation to humanity in the Lord Jesus Christ. We ask that you have mercy on us through Jesus Christ our Saviour who knew you perfectly as both Father and Lord.

Lord God, we acknowledge that our way of living as your people has been inadequate and that in this area we have misused your name. We have made great promises with our mouths and yet failed to deliver them in our lives. We have been delighted to have the privileges of being your children, yet we have ducked the responsibilities of being sons and daughters of God. We confess that in many ways we have dishonoured your name in our lives. We ask that you have mercy upon us, through Jesus Christ who lived the life that we should live in order to bring us to eternal life.

Lord God, we acknowledge that our way of worshipping you has been inadequate and that in this area too we have misused your name. We have failed time and time again to deal with you in the way that is right and proper. We have been commanded to love you with all our heart, soul and mind and we have not done this. So often we have sung, said or prayed things in your name that have fallen far short of what they should be. We ask that you have mercy upon us, through Jesus Christ who did indeed worship you perfectly. Amen.

PRAYER OF COMMITMENT

Lord God, we acknowledge that our thinking about you has been inadequate. Grant us Lord the right balance of reverence and rejoicing, awe and affection, fear and familiarity that we would know you both as heavenly Father and as Almighty Lord.

Lord God, we acknowledge that our way of living as your people has been inadequate. Pray that our lives would bring your name honour, not shame. Show us the way to live and give us the power to live that way through your Holy Spirit.

Lord God, we acknowledge that our way of worshipping you has been inadequate. Help us, from now on, as individuals and as a church, to worship you properly in spirit and in truth.

Bring glory to your name through all we think, do and say.

For we ask this in the name of Jesus Christ, Amen.

Don't Make Idols!

Commandment 2: Exodus 20:4–6 'Do not make idols of any kind, whether in the shape of birds or animals or fish. You must never worship or bow down to them, for I, the LORD your God, am a jealous God who will not share your affection with any other god! I do not leave unpunished the sins of those who hate me, but I punish the children for the sins of their parents to the third and fourth generations. But I lavish my love on those who love me and obey my commands, even for a thousand generations.'

[Note: At first glance there seems little in this commandment to give offence to the average church congregation today. The fact is that when we look more deeply at what this commandment really means we see that it still bites – and bites hard – today. You may find that your listeners are more offended by the application of this command-ment than many of the others. You have been warned!]

1) SUGGESTED HYMNS AND SONGS

HYMNS
- When I survey the wondrous cross
- O for a closer walk with God
- Facing a task unfinished
- Jesus call us: o'er the tumult
- The Lord is King, let Earth be glad

SONGS
- Heart of worship [Matt Redman]

- Ah Lord God
- As the deer pants for the water
- Faithful one so unchanging
- I will build my church
- Great is the Lord and most worthy of praise.
- Lamb of God; Holy One

2) WARM-UP ACTIVITIES & ILLUSTRATIONS

PARTICIPATORY QUESTIONS

These are a series of questions (to which there are no right answers) which are meant to focus people's thinking on the issues that lie at the core of our lives.

1) What do people do today when they need...

- Cheering up?
- Reassuring?
- Guidance?
- A change?

2) What do people today look forward to?
[Note: You ought to be able to draw out the fact that many people spend their lives looking forward to holidays, weekends, Christmas parties, etc.]

3) You sometimes hear it said of people that they 'live for' something. What we mean by this is that their lives centre on this particular pleasure, pastime or profession. Without naming individuals, what sort of things have you come across that people live for?

3) CHILDREN'S ACTIVITY

PREPARATIONS

You will need a large, cheap and (for best effect) ludicrous inflatable object, that imitates something like a dog, cat or a household item such as a hammer. It is the sort of thing that you can readily buy from a market or pound shop.

ACTIVITY
Bring out your object in already-inflated state. Say how wonderful you think it is. Describe, with imagination and feeling, how much better it is than the real thing. Give your reasons. For example: an inflatable dog is useful because it needs no walking, makes no mess, eats no food, etc.

Ask the children to agree. Hopefully some will dissent. Draw out why they disagree. What are the disadvantages? Try to get them to point out that whatever it is, it's not as good as the real thing!

As you are doing this, try to unobtrusively remove the stopper on the inflatable object (or put a pin in it!) so that the object deflates leaving you looking embarrassed.

CONCLUSION
Point out that the teaching today is about idols. 'Do not make idols of any kind, whether in the shape of birds or animals or fish. You must never worship or bow down to them.' An idol is something that pretends to be God but which isn't. It is an imitation God. It can be a thing (money) or it can be a person (a pop star or a footballer) or it can be a way of spending our time (watching a football team, or shopping).

Idols are like the inflatable object. They have some advantages; they are cheaper and less demanding, but where it counts they just don't work. They can't hear our prayers, they cannot guide us and they cannot get us to heaven. God, by contrast, is real; he helps us and cares for us but he requires that we serve him.

Point out that we must be very careful that what we fill our lives with is not a useless idol.

4) BIBLE READINGS

OLD TESTAMENT
Exodus 32:4–14

CAST
Introducer
Text Narrator
The People: Several voices; in their first line they should have a rather irritated edge to their tone
The LORD: Must sound annoyed
Moses: Should sound genuinely concerned

Introducer: After Moses had led the Israelites out of Egypt, God summoned him up on Mount Sinai where he received the Ten Commandments. Meanwhile, down at the foot of the mountain the Israelites waited. And waited...

Text Narrator: When Moses failed to come back down the mountain right away, the people went to Aaron.

The People: Look make us some gods who can lead us. This man Moses, who brought us here from Egypt, has disappeared. We don't know what has happened to him.

Text Narrator: So Aaron said...

Aaron: Tell your wives and sons and daughters to take off their gold earrings, and then bring them to me.

Text Narrator: All the people obeyed Aaron and brought him their gold earrings. Then Aaron took the gold, melted it down, and moulded and tooled it into the shape of a calf. Then the people exclaimed...

The People: O Israel, these are the gods who brought you out of Egypt!

Text Narrator: When Aaron saw how excited the people were about it, he built an altar in front of the calf and announced…

Aaron: Tomorrow there will be a festival to the LORD!

Text Narrator: So the people got up early the next morning to sacrifice burnt offerings and peace offerings. After this, they celebrated with feasting and drinking, and indulged themselves in pagan revelry. Then the LORD told Moses,

The LORD: Quick! Go down the mountain! The people you brought from Egypt have defiled themselves. They have already turned from the way I commanded them to live. They have made an idol shaped like a calf, and they have worshipped and sacrificed to it. They are saying, 'These are your gods, O Israel, who brought you out of Egypt'. I have seen how stubborn and rebellious these people are. Now leave me alone so my anger can blaze against them and destroy them all. Then I will make you, Moses, into a great nation instead of them.

Text Narrator: But Moses pleaded with the LORD his God…

Moses: O LORD! Why are you so angry with your own people whom you brought from the land of Egypt with such great power and mighty acts? The Egyptians will say, 'God tricked them into coming to the mountains so he could kill them and wipe them from the face of the earth.' Turn away from your fierce anger. Change your mind about this terrible disaster you are planning against your people! Remember your covenant with your servants – Abraham, Isaac, and Jacob. You swore by your own self, 'I will make your descendants as numerous as the stars of heaven. Yes, I will give them all of this land that I have promised to your descendants, and they will possess it forever.'

Text Narrator: So the LORD withdrew his threat and didn't bring against his people the disaster he had threatened.

(Exodus 32:4–14)

Isaiah 44:6–20

CAST
Introducer
Isaiah: Should be someone who is good at biting sarcasm (every church has at least one such person!)
The LORD: As elsewhere

Isaiah: This is what the LORD, Israel's King and Redeemer, the LORD Almighty, says:

The LORD: I am the First and the Last; there is no other God. Who else can tell you what is going to happen in the days ahead? Let them tell you if they can and thus prove their power. Let them do as I have done since ancient times. Do not tremble; do not be afraid. Have I not proclaimed from ages past what my purposes are for you? You are my witnesses – is there any other God? No! There is no other Rock – not one!

Isaiah: How foolish are those who manufacture idols to be their gods. These highly valued objects are really worthless. They themselves are witnesses that this is so, for their idols neither see nor know. No wonder those who worship them are put to shame. Who but a fool would make his own god – an idol that cannot help him one bit! All who worship idols will stand before the LORD in shame, along with all these craftsmen – mere humans – who claim they can make a god. Together they will stand in terror and shame.

The blacksmith stands at his forge to make a sharp tool, pounding and shaping it with all his might. His work makes him hungry and thirsty, weak and faint. Then the wood-carver measures and marks out a block of wood, takes the tool, and carves the figure of a man. Now he has a wonderful idol that cannot even move from where it is placed! He cuts down cedars; he selects the cypress and the oak; he plants the cedar in the forest to be nourished by the rain. And after his care, he uses part of the wood to make a fire to warm himself and bake his bread. Then – yes, it's true – he takes the rest of it and makes himself a god for people to worship! He makes an idol and bows down and praises it! He burns part of the tree to roast his meat and to keep himself warm. Then he takes what's left and makes his god: a carved idol! He falls down in front of it, worshipping and praying to it. 'Rescue me!' he says. 'You are my god!'

Such stupidity and ignorance! Their eyes are closed, and they cannot see. Their minds are shut, and they cannot think. The person who made the idol never stops to reflect, 'Why, it's just a block of wood! I burned half of it for heat and used it to bake my bread and roast my meat. How can the rest of it be a god? Should I bow down to worship a chunk of wood?' The poor, deluded fool feeds on ashes. He is trusting something that can give him no help at all. Yet he cannot bring himself to ask, 'Is this thing, this idol that I'm holding in my hand, a lie?'

The Psalms

Either Psalm 24 or Psalm 115:1–8. These are probably best done as single-voice readings.

(a) Psalm 24

CAST
Introducer
Reader

Introducer: Psalm 24 talks about the privilege of being able to stand before God and to enter his presence. One condition for us to come to God is to be free from idolatry.

Reader:
> The earth is the LORD's, and everything in it.
> The world and all its people belong to him.
> For he laid the earth's foundation on the seas
> and built it on the ocean depths.
> Who may climb the mountain of the LORD?
> Who may stand in his holy place?
> Only those whose hands and hearts are pure,
> who do not worship idols
> and never tell lies.
> They will receive the LORD's blessing
> and have right standing with God their saviour.
> They alone may enter God's presence
> and worship the God of Israel.
>
> Open up, ancient gates!
> Open up, ancient doors,
> and let the King of glory enter.
> Who is the King of glory?
> The LORD, strong and mighty,
> the LORD, invincible in battle.
> Open up, ancient gates!
> Open up, ancient doors,
> and let the King of glory enter.
> Who is the King of glory?
> The LORD Almighty –
> he is the King of glory.

(Psalm 24)

Or

Psalm 115:1–8

Introducer: One of the classic passages in the Bible on the folly of idolatry is Psalm 115. Here the writer encourages the people of Israel to worship God, pointing out as he does how pathetic it is to worship idols.

Reader:
Not to us, O LORD, but to you goes all the glory
for your unfailing love and faithfulness.
Why let the nations say,
'Where is their God?'
For our God is in the heavens
and he does as he wishes.
Their idols are merely things of silver and gold,
shaped by human hands.
They cannot talk, though they have mouths,
or see, though they have eyes!
They cannot hear with their ears,
or smell with their noses,
or feel with their hands,
or walk with their feet,
or utter sounds with their throats!
And those who make them are just like them,
as are all who trust in them.

(Psalm 115:1–8)

NEW TESTAMENT
[Note: these three sets of readings deal respectively with three types of idolatry discussed in the sermon.]

Acts 17:16–34 or Romans 1:18–22

(a) Acts 17:16–34

CAST
Introducer
Text Narrator
Paul
Philosophers: Two groups; both scornful at the start but one less so at the end

Introducer: By the time of the New Testament, on the surface at least, idolatry was extinct in Israel. The Jews worshipped no statues or images and they despised those people such as the Romans who did. In fact it was only when the followers of Jesus went out into the world of the Greeks and Romans that they really came into confrontation with idols of wood and stone. In Chapter 17 of the Book of Acts, we read how, after trouble in Berea, Paul was forced to move on. He went to Athens where he decided to wait for his companions, Silas and Timothy, to join him.

Text Narrator: While Paul was waiting for Silas and Timothy in Athens, he was deeply troubled by all the idols he saw everywhere in the city. He went to the synagogue to debate with the Jews and the God-fearing Gentiles, and he spoke daily in the public square to all who happened to be there. He also had a debate with some of the Epicurean and Stoic philosophers. When he told them about Jesus and his resurrection, they said...

Philosophers 1: This babbler has picked up some strange ideas.

Text Narrator: Others said...

Philosophers 2: He's pushing some foreign religion.

Text Narrator: Then they took him to the Council of Philosophers, saying...

Philosophers 1 & 2: Come and tell us more about this new religion. You are saying some rather startling things, and we want to know what it's all about.

Text Narrator: It should be explained that all the Athenians as well as the foreigners in Athens seemed to spend all their time discussing the latest ideas. So Paul, standing before the Council, addressed them as follows...

Paul: Men of Athens, I notice that you are very religious, for as I was walking along I saw your many altars. And one of them had this inscription on it: 'To an Unknown God.' You have been worshiping him without knowing who he is, and now I wish to tell you about him.

He is the God who made the world and everything in it. Since he is Lord of heaven and earth, he doesn't live in man-made temples, and human hands can't serve his needs – for he has no needs. He himself gives life and breath to everything, and he satisfies every need there is. From one man he created all the nations throughout the whole earth. He decided beforehand which should rise and fall, and he determined their boundaries. His purpose in all of this was that the nations should seek after God and perhaps feel their way toward him and find him – though he is not far from any one of us. For in him we live and move and exist. As one of your own poets says, 'We are his offspring.' And since this is true, we shouldn't think of God as an idol designed by craftsmen from gold or silver or stone. God overlooked people's former ignorance about these things, but now he commands everyone everywhere to turn away from idols and turn to him. For he has set a day for judging the world with justice by the man he has appointed, and he proved to everyone who this is by raising him from the dead.

Text Narrator: When they heard Paul speak of the resurrection of a person who had been dead, some laughed...

Philosophers 1: *[Can make scornful noises such as Pah! Huh! Really!]*

Text Narrator: But others said...

Philosophers 2: We want to hear more about this later.

Text Narrator: That ended Paul's discussion with them, but some joined him and became believers. Among them were Dionysius, a member of the Council, a woman named Damaris, and others.

(Acts 17:16–34)

Or

(b) Romans 1:18–25
[Note: This passage, of course, touches on the issue of homosexuality. Dealing with this and idolatry in the same service without doing an injustice to the issues surrounding either is hardly feasible.]

CAST
Introducer
Paul

Introducer: In the New Testament the most thorough statement on idolatry and its consequences, is found in the first chapter of Romans.

Paul: But God shows his anger from heaven against all sinful, wicked people who push the truth away from themselves. For the truth about God is known to them instinctively. God has put this knowledge in their hearts. From the time the world was created, people have seen the earth and sky and all that God made. They can clearly see his invisible qualities – his eternal power and divine nature. So they have no excuse whatsoever for not knowing God.

Yes, they knew God, but they wouldn't worship him as God or even give him thanks. And they began to think up foolish ideas of what God was like. The result was that their minds became dark and confused. Claiming to be wise, they became utter fools instead. And instead of worshipping the glorious, ever-living God, they worshipped idols made to look like mere people, or birds and animals and snakes.

So God let them go ahead and do whatever shameful things their hearts desired. As a result, they did vile and degrading things with each other's bodies. Instead of believing what they knew was the truth about God, they deliberately chose to believe lies. So they worshipped the things God made but not the Creator himself, who is to be praised forever. Amen.

Matthew 6:24 and Colossians 3:5

CAST
Introducer
Jesus
Paul

Introducer: But there are many levels to idolatry. Even without statues, idolatry of things is possible. Jesus himself warned…

Jesus: No one can serve two masters. For you will hate one and love the other, or be devoted to one and despise the other. You cannot serve both God and money.

Introducer: And Paul, writing to the Colossian church, was equally strong.

Paul: So put to death the sinful, earthly things lurking within you. Have nothing to do with sexual sin, impurity, lust, and shameful desires. Don't be greedy for the good things of this life, for that is idolatry.

John 11:45–53

CAST
Introducer
Text Narrator: The final line ('from that time on the Jewish leaders began to plot Jesus' death') should be delivered with a tone of appalled horror
Religious Leaders: Bewildered and worried
Caiaphas: Arrogant and confident

Introducer: But there is still another level of idolatry; and this is the subtlest and most deadly kind of all. Here what is worshipped in place of God is not things that can be touched like statues or money, it is invisible things like one's country, one's traditions or even, most terrible of all, one's religion. In John's gospel we read how, after the raising from the dead of Lazarus, the Jewish religious leaders – the Sanhedrin – were faced with the challenge of what they were to do with Jesus.

Text Narrator: Many of the people who were with Mary believed in Jesus when they saw this happen. But some went to the Pharisees and told them what Jesus had done. Then the leading priests and Pharisees called the high council together to discuss the situation.

Religious Leaders: What are we going to do? This man certainly performs many miraculous signs. If we leave him alone, the whole nation will follow him, and then the Roman army will come and destroy both our Temple and our nation.

Text Narrator: Then one of them, Caiaphas, who was high priest that year, said...

Caiaphas: How can you be so stupid? Why should the whole nation be destroyed? Let this one man die for the people.

Text Narrator: This prophecy that Jesus should die for the entire nation came from Caiaphas in his position as high priest. He didn't think of it himself; he was inspired to say it. It was a prediction that Jesus' death would be not for Israel only, but for the gathering together of all the children of God scattered around the world. So from that time on the Jewish leaders began to plot Jesus' death.

5) POEM BY STEWART HENDERSON

Adoration, veneration,
from such a holy place.
Difficult to keep pristine
but easy to deface.

Supplication, exaltation;
beguiled priorities,
your acts of consummation
with quicksand forgeries.

Imitation, simulation
and emulatory.
Though idols have their moments,
I Am Eternity.

What counterfeit can promise you
a new, unsullied start?
So yield to me my blemished love,
betroth your damaged heart.

6) SERMON

IDOLATRY OR TRUE WORSHIP?

Commandment 2: Exodus 20:4–6 'Do not make idols of any kind, whether in the shape of birds or animals or fish. You must never worship or bow down to them, for I, the LORD your God, am a jealous God who will not share your affection with any other god! I do not leave unpunished the sins of those who hate me, but I punish the children for the sins of their parents to the third and fourth generations. But I lavish my love on those who love me and obey my commands, even for a thousand generations.'

INTRODUCTION

To announce that you are going to preach on idolatry to a 21st-century Western congregation is to risk being greeted by a great sigh of relief. Idolatry, we all know, is a Stone Age crime. It is something to be commented on by archaeologists and anthropologists; it belongs to the past and it is something that we have evolved beyond. We can relax.

But can we? As has been widely pointed out, *homo sapiens* is a species with a deeply ingrained habit of worshipping. It is all too easy for our hearts, minds and lives to find something else other than the one true and living God to bow down before. As we shall see the only thing that has really changed over thousands of years is the way in which we commit idolatry.

In fact the peril of idolatry should surprise no careful reader of the Bible; after all there are more references to this second commandment in its pages than to any of the other nine.

It is useful to divide idols into two types; those whose power comes from our longing for them and those whose power is derived from our fear of them. Sadly both types are alive and well today.

IDOLS THAT WE LONG FOR

When we think seriously about this kind of idol we find that within it there are at least three different types. In the absence of better terms we can call these made idols, market place idols and mental idols. Let us look at each in turn.

Made idols

By 'made idols' we mean physical objects that have been produced to be worshipped. These are the sort of thing that became such a problem to the people of Israel in the Old Testament and that Paul became so indignant about in Athens. They include such things as those bronze or carved marble and wood statues to which sacrifices are offered. These made idols are either assumed to be God (or gods), or to be images or representations of him (or her, it or them). Whatever the precise rationalization, it is these objects that people either physically or mentally bow down before. Many religions in the world today have such images and it is naive (and probably offensive) to think that they are a mark of a 'primitive culture'. After all, the idolatrous Greeks of Athens whom Paul encountered in Acts 15 were some of the most highly educated people of their day.

If relatively few people in Britain have made idols that they worship then many more carry lucky charms or talismans. While these may not be actually worshipped the idea that things, rather than God himself, bring blessing is surely a breach of this commandment. It is a reminder that no visible boundary lies between superstition and idolatry.

Now, it would be easy to spend time discussing made idols but it is important to move on quickly; there are more subtle forms of idolatry around.

[Note: There are issues here that need to be either handled sensitively or nimbly dodged. For example, ever since the Reformation there has been a heated debate over whether the icons or images widely present in the Orthodox and Catholic Churches are actually worshipped or whether they are merely aids to worship. An equally

delicate area is the extent to which non-Christian religions are guilty of idolatry. Muslims, for instance, with their strict ban against any visual depiction of Allah or Mohammed, feel that it is Christians, not they, who break this commandment.]

Market place idols

One of the main problems with idolatry is that when we think of it, we think mainly in terms of made idols. This commandment, we tell ourselves, is directed to those who offer incense to carved stone gods and goddesses in the middle of steaming jungles. It does not apply to us. Of course, if idolatry was made a crime and the police were given a warrant to search our houses for idols, few of us would be convicted.

But, as with the other sins addressed in these commandments, there are hidden depths to idolatry. The danger with idolatry is to define an idol purely on its form: to say that for something to be an idol, it has to be such a shape and such a size. It is far wiser (and easier) to define an idol in terms of function; what it does in our lives rather than what it is. Ultimately, the function of an idol is to replace God. So, for example, an idol is anything that we allow to give the purpose, meaning and fulfilment to our lives that only God can give. An idol is anything that replaces God as the central focus around which our lives revolve. God ought to dominate and control every major area of our lives; what we hope, what we fear, what we honour and how we make our decisions. An idol is anything that has edged God out in these areas.

Now when we think of idols in those terms we realise that there are many day-to-day things that can become idols. These can be called market place idols; they are the things that we buy or sell and talk about every day without even thinking that they may be connected with idolatry. Some of these market place idols are things that we can touch and see; others are less visible. Most obvious of all of these is money with its claims to bring peace of mind and joy of heart to the possessor. But close behind it are other material things; cars, computers, houses, food and so on. The creaking shelves of our local newsagents are stocked with magazines that reflect the insatiable hunger for people to fill their lives with material things.

In terms of our culture, the market place idols are well expressed by what we build. Here what we worship is expressed (very literally) in concrete terms. Many people have described our modern-day shopping malls and out-of-town retail parks as the cathedrals of our time. There are also the other great constructions devoted to pleasure; the cinemas, night clubs, restaurants and sports centres. And of course there are also the many places devoted to the most cherished of all these idols; our bodies. The health centres, hairdressers, beauty salons, sports clubs all reflect a preoccupation with fitness and beauty.

Let me point out two specific market place idols of our time. One of these is security. In order to try to possess security, that elusive freedom from worry, people accumulate money, houses, pension and health schemes. Yet oddly enough, however great the sacrifices, security and peace of mind seem to escape them.

Other market place idols centre on leisure and holidays; both of which are now billion pound industries. The significance of leisure to people today is striking; for many, this is really what the world is all about. You hear people say 'I am only really alive when I am clubbing' (or climbing, canoeing or a thousand other things). Others boast that they only work so that they can enjoy the weekends. Holidays, too, have assumed an extraordinary prominence in the national psyche. It has been cynically said that our ancestors went on pilgrimages to be blessed and to get closer to heaven. Apparently for much the same motives today we go on holidays.

Now of course most of these things that form market place idols are good. But then it is always the best things that make the most dangerous idols. Health is good, beauty is good, leisure is good, pleasure is good, possessions are good. No one is in favour of illness, ugliness, overwork, boredom and poverty. But it is when these things get out of proportion that the trouble begins; the danger is when they go from being good to being gods.

And as we shall see like the inflatable dog *[or whatever was used in the children's talk]* these market place idols are a pathetic and ultimately worthless substitute for the reality that is God.

Mental idols

If there are made idols and market place idols, there is a third class of idols. We can call these 'mental idols' and among them are some of the most dangerous idols of all.

Mental idols are beliefs or ideas that get in the way or replace our worship of God. Let me briefly list some.

For many people the ultimate meaning of life is to be found in Culture. The heart of what it is to be human is to be found in concert halls, art galleries or within the pages of great literature. For others it is Philosophy or Education that is the centre of what we are as a species. Here the universities become our temples and learning is our religion.

For others it is Science or Technology that is the hope of the world. Listen to such people talking about, say, the future of the Internet and you will hear talk of better worlds with a hope and zeal that seem lifted straight from the Bible.

For still more people, Patriotism or Nationalism has become the centre of existence, providing meaning, purpose and morality to their life. Here the Fatherland, the Nation or the language has taken on a god-like quality. And, as our war memorials show, sometimes these mental idols have a taste for blood sacrifices.

For yet others the Environment has become a God, setting out its own stern moral demands and with its own collection of doom-announcing prophets.

Of course as with the market place idols the tragedy is that what is worshipped are good things, not bad. There is the thinnest of lines between the legitimate honouring of what is good and the illegitimate worshipping of the same thing. Christians are, of course, in favour of culture, education, science, the environment and the rest. But they must have their place and that place is not on the throne of God.

Yet within these mental idols there is one that we have not mentioned that is perhaps the deadliest of them all. It is that which occurs within religion. Here what typically happens is that God genuinely blesses a church, a denomination or an individual in some way. But, as time passes, the object or the means through which the blessing occurred, acquires an almost divine status. Eventually the focus of worship becomes not the one, true and living God, Father, Son and Holy Spirit, but the object or means. There are classic instances in the Bible. For example we read in Numbers 21 how, when the children of Israel were in the wilderness and grumbling against God he sent poisonous snakes amongst them. When they repented, God told Moses to make a bronze replica snake and to put it on a pole so that those who looked at it would be healed. It appears that this image was preserved in the temple because centuries later King Hezekiah had to destroy it because 'the people of Israel had begun to worship it by burning incense to it'. (2 Kings 18:4.)

Similar idolatry has happened ever since, whether it is with hymnbooks, church buildings, service formats or preaching styles. It has even – terrible though it is to say it – occurred with theologies.

The passage from John's gospel (John 11:45–53) that we read earlier provides what is, in many ways, the ultimate example of this sort of idolatry. Here we read that, alarmed by the popularity that Jesus had after the raising of Lazarus, the Jewish religious council – the Sanhedrin – met to decide what to do with him. They were concerned that if his popularity rose higher there might be an uprising that would result in the destruction by the Romans of their temple, religion and nation. As Caiaphas pointed out, the choice was plain; it was one man or the system. And so they decided to destroy the one man. When faced with a choice between Jesus – God amongst them – or a religious system that merely pointed to God, the system won. In fact as history tells us, it was a terrible mistake. Not only did the crucifixion not end Jesus' influence but within a generation the Romans had done precisely all that they had feared and the temple was totally destroyed.

Some of the most deadly idolatry in religion does not occur with statues or icons. It is invisible and lies purely in our minds. We must be very careful that we do not create idols within our own church systems that stand in the way of God.

IDOLS THAT WE FEAR

The idols that we have just thought about are the idols whose power over us comes because we desire them or what they offer. We serve them because they dangle a carrot of promise in front of us.

But not all idols are served out of desire. After all, think of the terrible pagan gods that demanded human sacrifice; they were reverenced out of fear rather than affection. Christianity has coloured the English language; the words we use for dealing with God such as 'adore', 'worship' and 'idolize' all have positive overtones. Among pagans whose gods were cruel and unloving, worship was a fearsome business.

These idols still exist. These are the idols that we are frightened of; the powers and forces that force us to serve them because, if we do not, we believe something terrible will happen to us. These are the idols that drive us not by the carrot of promise but with the stick of fear.

Fear is a powerful motivating force. It was doubtless the fear of starvation or conquest that drove the nation of Israel to serve false gods in the Old Testament as much as a desire for them. Certainly fear of the Romans helped drive Caiaphas and the Sanhedrin into deciding to execute Jesus. And fear drives us to deny God even today.

Let us list some imaginary cases where fear has stopped people from doing what is right:

- Fear of unemployment causes Dave to agree to his boss's tax fraud

- Fear of being bullied herself causes Karen to look the other way when a girl in her class is being punched
- Fear of being laughed at stops Max from talking about his Christian faith at work
- Fear of being single for the rest of her life causes Liz to agree to marry someone whom she knows is not God's choice for her
- Fear of an old age spent in poverty stops Rick from giving up his business job and obeying God's calling to go into the ministry

The list could go on. And privately we need to look hard into our own lives to see what examples we can find there where fear has stopped us from doing good. We need to ask God to show us what forces there are that enslave us and we need to ask him to set us free.

THE ANTIDOTES TO IDOLATRY
Idolatry is wrong. So how are we to deal with it? Let me make five suggestions.

Realise that idolatry is attractive

The first suggestion is for us to frankly realise that idolatry in some shape or form is always a danger. Idolatry is, in fact, surprisingly attractive. This may seem odd; after all why would anyone choose (in Paul's words of Romans 1:23) to exchange the worship of 'the glorious, ever-living God' for 'idols made to look like mere people, or birds and animals and snakes'?

One part of the answer lies in the terrible mystery of sin; in rejecting God we somehow end up accepting idols instead. As worshipping creatures we have to worship something; if you remove God then other things must fill the vacuum.

Another part of the attraction of idols can be seen in the illustration of the inflatable dog [or whatever the item was] in the children's sketch earlier. There is, on the surface, something undemanding about idols. They do not answer back, they do not make moral demands and we can feel that we remain in control. Idols are tame gods and – in theory at least – we can take an axe to them at any time. But, of course, this is lies, because idols worm their roots so deep down into our hearts that it needs major surgery to remove them.

We need to be wary. Scripture tells us that, although Solomon was the wisest of men, in his old age he fell into idolatry (1 Kings 11:4). And if it can happen to Solomon it can happen to any of us.

Recognise your own idols

We need to engage in some careful self-examination. Do we have idols and where do they lie? There are various ways of finding out. It has been said that we can tell what we worship by watching what our minds drift into thinking about in quiet moments. There is something in this; when our minds are in neutral our thoughts will automatically gravitate towards what is the centre of our lives. If, whenever you are stuck in a traffic jam, or waiting in a queue to use the photocopier, or just lying awake at night, you find that your mind repeatedly drifts towards holidays, buying clothes, or football then it is these things that are the idols you are attracted too. Equally if your mind is constantly nagged by some fear, perhaps of illness or rejection, then it may be that it is these, not God, that lie at the real core of your lives.

Painful though it may be, we need to recognise what idols we, as individuals, are tempted towards worshipping. Only then can we deal with them.

Realise that idolatry insults God

The second commandment says this about idols, 'You must never worship or bow down to them, for I, the LORD your God, am a jealous God who will not share your affection with any other god!'

God says plainly that, when it comes to our worship, he is

a jealous God. He wants all of our worship; not just a small part of it. He will accept being Lord of our lives but only of all of our lives and not of a part. And if you think about it, you can see why. If my life revolves around money then for God to agree to being my Lord on a time-share basis (say three hours every Sunday) would be for him to allow himself to be on the same level as money. We would be asking God to take an equal position with dull, lifeless lumps of metal. We deeply insult God by asking him to coexist in our hearts with things.

We need to realise that God is hurt and offended by our idolatry. He will either be Lord of all that we are, or not at all.

Realise that idolatry betrays us

But we also need to realise that we are the chief loser when we engage in idolatry. Idols can do nothing for us. As Isaiah and the other prophets pointed out, idols are blind and cannot see our needs, deaf and cannot hear our prayers, stupid and cannot understand our predicament and powerless to help us anyway. Dealing with an idol is about as much use as talking down a phone that has been cut off.

In fact, not only do idols not do anything good for us they can also betray us. They pretend to be harmless, amiable creatures that we can control but very soon we find that they are the masters of our lives that we cannot get rid of.

These four antidotes to idolatry that I have suggested are all negative. The last however is very positive.

Remember the power of praise

In the Old Testament there is a great deal about idolatry. But there is even more about how the Lord is to be praised. This is the key to defeating idolatry. After all if we have spent time seriously praising God for who he is and what he has done, then we are far less likely to be either wooed or frightened by idols. When we have been reminding ourselves that God is all-powerful, all-wise and ever-living we are far more likely to be able to look at the temptations of money, fame or pleasure and laugh in their face.

Praise reminds us who God really is and it is the best antidote to idolatry.

CONCLUSION

As we have seen it is an act of foolishness to deny the presence or power of idolatry today. Idols occur in a thousand forms and we all face idolatry as a danger in almost every area of life. Ironically, the risk of idolatry is greatest with things that are good and important.

What this commandment says is that we need to be sure that the only person or force controlling our behaviour is God himself. It is all too easy for us to be enticed away from doing what is right by wrong desires. That is idolatry. It is equally easy for us to be scared away from doing right by our fears; that too is idolatry.

We need to realise that God – and God alone – is the one who should be the centre of our lives. Only he can satisfy the desires of our hearts and he alone is the one we should fear.

Towards the end of a long life the apostle John wrote the letter that we call First John. At the very close of that letter he makes an appeal to the church: 'Dear children, keep yourselves from idols.' (1 John 5:21, NIV.)

That appeal echoes on down through the centuries to our own day. Until Jesus comes we will continue to need to be reminded that idolatry is a threat and that we need to keep ourselves from idols.

7) SUGGESTED PRAYERS

PRAYER OF CONFESSION

Lord God, Father, Son and Holy Spirit, we acknowledge that you alone are to be worshipped. There is no one like you, Lord God, creator, sustainer and redeemer of the world. To you alone belongs eternal praise, honour, glory and worship.

We would ask, Lord God, that you would shine the light of

your Holy Spirit into our lives that we would see plainly where we have sinned in putting other things before you. Reveal to us the idols in our lives. Grant us the grace to admit our idolatry, the desire to reject our idols and the strength to turn from them.

Where we have bowed down before idols and praised them instead of you, we ask your forgiveness. Have mercy upon us, O Lord our God.

Where we have allowed our lives to become obsessed by the idols of our world and have longed for what they have claimed to offer us we ask your forgiveness. Have mercy upon us, O Lord our God.

Where we have allowed our minds to become obsessed by the idols of our imagination and have treated ideas as gods we ask your forgiveness. Have mercy upon us, O Lord our God.

Father God, we confess that, all too often, we have let fear stop us from doing what is right. We have allowed ourselves in many ways to be intimidated by idols and as a result we have bowed to pressure and committed sin. We ask your forgiveness. Have mercy upon us, O Lord our God.

PRAYER OF COMMITMENT

Lord God, we would ask that you would now empower us through your Holy Spirit that we would be able to walk the right way in the days ahead. Grant us the ability to discern all temptations to idolatry. Give to us Lord, the desire and the ability to deal ruthlessly with those idols that we encounter in our hearts. May we be willing to eject them from our lives.

We especially bring to you those idols of fear whose dark shadows scare us from doing good and who often drive us into doing evil. Give us courage, an awareness of your great power and a knowledge of your Spirit's presence so that we can overcome fear. May we be those people whose reverent and loving fear for you drives out all other fears.

Encourage us Lord to continually praise you and give you honour and glory that, by always magnifying your holy name, we would put into perspective all those things that seek to take your place in our lives.

Help us Lord, to live our lives in single-minded devotion to you, Father, Son and Holy Spirit, through Jesus Christ our Lord, Amen.

Commandment 1: Exodus 20:1–3 'Then God instructed the people as follows: "I am the LORD your God, who rescued you from slavery in Egypt. Do not worship any other gods besides me."'

[Note: This First Commandment forms the basis of the entire Ten Commandments; how we treat this commandment will affect how we treat all the others. The thrust of this service then is not simply towards the keeping of this commandment, it is towards our attitudes to all of them.]

1) SUGGESTED HYMNS AND SONGS

HYMNS
- In full and glad surrender
- This is the truth which we proclaim
- A debtor to mercy alone
- All people that on earth do dwell
- Before Jehovah's aweful throne (numerous variants exist)
- Give to our God immortal praise
- Crown Him with many crowns

SONGS
- Heart of worship [Matt Redman]
- Make way, make way
- Great is the Lord and most worthy of praise
- Holy, holy, holy is the Lord
- From the sun's rising unto the sun's setting

2) WARM-UP ACTIVITIES AND ILLUSTRATIONS

Announce that as we're going to think about the First Commandment today the first thing we're going to do is discuss weddings. Think about a traditional old-fashioned church wedding.

Question: Other than the people organising the wedding and the spectators, who is the wedding service for?

[Note: Draw out that a wedding centres on two people.]

Question: What are they doing in the service?

[Note: Draw out that they are making an agreement or contract between the two of them.]

Question: So is it like buying carpets? Or hiring a car? What sort of agreement is it?

[Note: Draw out that this is a life-time agreement or contract between the couple.]

Question: Can either person be already married?

[Note: The point here is to make it plain that this is an exclusive arrangement. There cannot be a third party.]

Question: What does he promise?

[Note: Traditionally at least to 'love her, comfort her, honour, and keep her, in sickness and in health; and, forsaking all other, keep only unto her, so long as both shall live'.]

Question: What does she promise?

[Note: Traditionally at least 'to obey him, and serve him, love, honour, and keep him, in sickness and in health; and, forsaking all other, keep only unto him, so long as both shall live'. Don't get sidetracked on the obedience bit.]

Question: What is the proof of the wedding? What are the symbols of the completion of the wedding?

[Note: The certificate and the two rings.]

[Now summarise along the following lines.] In a marriage ceremony what we have is a public service where one man and one woman solemnly commit themselves to be bonded to each other for life. They make sworn agreements to each other of support and loyalty, sign a certificate and exchange symbols.

As we go on to look at the first commandment we will find that this image of marriage will help us understand what lies behind this commandment.

3) CHILDREN'S ACTIVITY

PREPARATIONS
Hidden near the front should be three things:

- A closed cardboard box with a slit cut inside the lid. Inside should be a toy frog or something equally ugly.
- A plastic bag with a few sweets inside that look like something inedible (snails, slugs or a snake?).
- A small screw-top bottle of fruit juice or pop. The seal around the cap should be broken as though you might have put something in it.

You ought to have a respectable bag of sweets as a reward.

ACTIVITY
Announce that you are going to ask for a volunteer but before anybody sticks their hands up you must explain to them what they have to do.

a) They will have to perform three tasks.
b) They will have to obey you. Totally!

- Pick a volunteer. Depending how confident he or she is, you can unnerve them by making asides to the others.
- Direct them to the box. 'Task one is to pull out what ever is in the box.'
- Then direct them to the bag. 'Task two is to eat whatever is in the box.'
- Then direct them to the bottle. 'Task three is to take a drink from whatever is in the bottle.'
- Reward them, give them a round of applause and get them to sit down.

CONCLUSION

Explain that what they have just seen was faith. It was trusting and obeying what someone else said in spite of the evidence.

Should you always obey someone?

[Note: Put in here a warning about being too trusting with strangers, etc.]

But why had you been obeyed?

The answer you hope to get is that the volunteer trusted you. Now draw out why you were trusted.

[Note: What you are looking for is two things: (a) they trusted you because they knew who you were and (b) they trusted you because they were familiar with what you had done in the past.]

Trust and obedience form the background to this first commandment. God is asking the people of Israel to trust him, to follow him and be obedient to him alone.

So that the people will trust him God tells them two things.

- First, God tells them who he is; he is the Lord. Now this is a very special name; not just Lord this or Lord that. It is a personal name.
- Secondly, he says 'look what I have done for you already. I have brought you safe out of Egypt'. He has proved himself.

God wants us to trust him today and to obey him and follow him; just like he wanted the people of Israel to do. And he has done for us the same thing he did for them.

- First, he has shown us who he is: he has said that if you want to see who I am like, I am like Jesus.
- Second, he says look what I have done for you already. I have died for you on the cross.

Trust me he says: look who I am and look what I have done. Because of Jesus we can trust God and trust him totally.

4) BIBLE READINGS

OLD TESTAMENT

There are three suggested Old Testament readings. The first two of these are the key passages that frame the giving of the Ten Commandments and the Book of the Law; Exodus 19:1 – 20:3 and Exodus 24:1–11. A third – and briefer – reading is the prophecy in Jeremiah 31 of the coming new covenant. This is the vital background to the New Testament reading.

Exodus 19:1 – 20:3 and Exodus 24:1–11

Both Exodus readings have the same cast.

CAST
Introducer: See comments in Service One
Text Narrator: See comments in Service One
The Lord: See comments in Service One
Moses
The people

Introducer: Under Moses' leadership God has led the Israelites out of Egypt and into the wilderness of Sinai.

Text Narrator: The Israelites arrived in the wilderness of Sinai exactly two months after they left Egypt. After breaking camp at Rephidim, they came to the base of Mount Sinai and set up camp there. Then Moses climbed the mountain to appear before God. The Lord called out to him from the mountain…

The Lord: Give these instructions to the descendants of Jacob, the people of Israel: 'You have seen what I did to the Egyptians. You know how I brought you to myself and carried you on eagle's wings. Now if you will obey me and keep my covenant, you will be my own special treasure from among all the nations of the earth; for all the earth belongs to me. And you will be to me a kingdom of priests, my holy nation.' Give this message to the Israelites.

Text Narrator: Moses returned from the mountain and called together the leaders of the people and told them what the Lord had said. They all responded together

The People: We will certainly do everything the Lord asks of us.

Text Narrator: So Moses brought the people's answer back to the Lord. Then the Lord said to Moses...

The Lord: I am going to come to you in a thick cloud so the people themselves can hear me as I speak to you. Then they will always have confidence in you.

Text Narrator: Moses told the Lord what the people had said. Then the Lord told Moses...

The Lord: Go down and prepare the people for my visit. Purify them today and tomorrow, and have them wash their clothing. Be sure they are ready on the third day, for I will come down upon Mount Sinai as all the people watch. Set boundary lines that the people may not pass. Warn them, 'Be careful! Do not go up on the mountain or even touch its boundaries. Those who do will certainly die! Any people or animals that cross the boundary must be stoned to death or shot with arrows. They must not be touched by human hands.' The people must stay away from the mountain until they hear one long blast from the ram's horn. Then they must gather at the foot of the mountain.

Text Narrator: So Moses went down to the people. He purified them for worship and had them wash their clothing. He told them...

Moses: Get ready for an important event two days from now. ['And until then, abstain from having sexual intercourse'. *Could replace this with* 'Purify yourselves'.]

Text Narrator: On the morning of the third day, there was a powerful storm with thunder and lightning, and a dense cloud came down upon the mountain. There was a long, loud blast from a ram's horn, and all the people trembled. Moses led them out from the camp to meet with God, and they stood at the foot of the mountain. All Mount Sinai was covered with smoke because the LORD had descended on it in the form of fire. The smoke billowed into the sky like smoke from a furnace, and the whole mountain shook with a violent earthquake. As the horn blast grew louder and louder, Moses spoke, and God thundered his reply for all to hear. The LORD came down on the top of Mount Sinai and called Moses to the top of the mountain. So Moses climbed the mountain. Then the LORD told Moses...

The LORD: Go back down and warn the people not to cross the boundaries. They must not come up here to see the LORD, for those who do will die. Even the priests who regularly come near to the LORD must purify themselves, or I will destroy them.

Moses: But, LORD, the people cannot come up on the mountain! You already told them not to. You told me to set boundaries around the mountain and to declare it off limits.

The LORD: Go down anyway and bring Aaron back with you. In the meantime, do not let the priests or the people cross the boundaries to come up here. If they do, I will punish them.

Text Narrator: So Moses went down to the people and told them what the LORD had said. Then God instructed the people as follows:

The LORD: I am the LORD your God, who rescued you from slavery in Egypt. Do not worship any other gods besides me.

(Exodus 19:1–20)

Introducer: After the LORD gave Israel the Ten Commandments at Mount Sinai he gave them various other laws that formed the Book of the Covenant and that are recorded in Exodus 21, 22 and 23. Finally the LORD gave Moses new instructions.

Text Narrator: Then the LORD instructed Moses...

The LORD: Come up here to me, and bring along Aaron, Nadab, Abihu, and seventy of Israel's leaders. All of them must worship at a distance. You alone, Moses, are allowed to come near to the LORD. The others must not come too close. And remember, none of the other people are allowed to climb on the mountain at all.

Text Narrator: When Moses had announced to the people all the teachings and regulations the LORD had given him, they answered in unison...

The People: We will do everything the LORD has told us to do.

Text Narrator: Then Moses carefully wrote down all the LORD's instructions. Early the next morning he built an altar at the foot of the mountain. He also set up twelve pillars around the altar, one for each of the twelve tribes of Israel. Then he sent some of the young men to sacrifice young bulls as burnt offerings and peace offerings to the LORD. Moses took half the blood from these animals and drew it off into basins. The other half he splashed against the altar.

Then he took the Book of the Covenant and read it to the people. They all responded again...

The People: We will do everything the LORD has commanded. We will obey.

Text Narrator: Then Moses sprinkled the blood from the basins over the people and said...

Moses: This blood confirms the covenant the LORD has made with you in giving you these laws.

Text Narrator: Then Moses, Aaron, Nadab, Abihu, and seventy of the leaders of Israel went up the mountain. There they saw the God of Israel. Under his feet there seemed to be a pavement of brilliant sapphire, as clear as the heavens. And though Israel's leaders saw God, he did not destroy them. In fact, they shared a meal together in God's presence!

(Exodus 24:1–11)

Jeremiah 31:31–34

CAST
Introducer
The Lord

Introducer: The Old Testament tells how the people of Israel frequently broke the covenant between them and the LORD by worshipping other gods. God, however, remained faithful. Long after the giving of the old covenant at Sinai, God announced through Jeremiah that one day there would be a new and superior covenant.

The LORD: The day will come when I will make a new covenant with the people of Israel and Judah. This covenant will not be like the one I made with their ancestors when I took them by the hand and brought them out of the land of Egypt. They broke that covenant, though I loved them as a husband loves his wife. But this is the new covenant I will make with the people of Israel on that day, I will put my laws in their minds, and I will write them on their hearts. I will be their God, and they will be my people. And they will not need to teach their neighbours, nor will they need to teach their family, saying, 'You should know the LORD.' For everyone, from the least to the greatest, will already know me. And I will forgive their wickedness and will never again remember their sins.

NEW TESTAMENT

Of the many readings that could be chosen here, three are suggested. These are Jesus' restatement of this commandment and two key references to the new covenant; Luke's account of the inauguration of the Last Supper and part of the treatment of this subject in the Epistle to the Hebrews. (If short of time this last can be omitted.)

Mark 12:28–34

CAST
Introducer
Text Narrator
Teacher of the Law
Jesus

Introducer: Jesus held that this first commandment was vital. One day, when Jesus was in discussion with Jewish religious leaders, the subject of the commandments came up.

Text Narrator: One of the teachers of religious law was standing there listening to the discussion. He realized that Jesus had answered well, so he asked...

Teacher of the Law: Of all the commandments, which is the most important?

Text Narrator: Jesus replied...

Jesus: The most important commandment is this: 'Hear, O Israel! The Lord our God is the one and only Lord. And you must love the Lord your God with all your heart, all your soul, all your mind, and all your strength.' The second is equally important: 'Love your neighbour as yourself.' No other commandment is greater than these.

Teacher of the Law: Well said, Teacher. You have spoken the truth by saying that there is only one God and no other. And I know it is important to love him with all my heart and all my understanding and all my strength, and to love my neighbours as myself. This is more important than to offer all of the burnt offerings and sacrifices required in the law.

Text Narrator: Realizing this man's understanding, Jesus said to him...

Jesus: You are not far from the Kingdom of God.

(Mark 12:28–34)

Luke 22:19–23

CAST
Introducer
Text Narrator
Jesus

Introducer: The theme of Jeremiah's prophecy, the new covenant lies at the heart of Jesus' ministry. He most plainly speaks of it on the night before the cross, when, with his disciples, he shared the meal that we have come to call the Last Supper.

Text Narrator: Then he took a loaf of bread; and when he had thanked God for it, he broke it in pieces and gave it to the disciples, saying,

Jesus: This is my body, given for you. Do this in remembrance of me.

Text Narrator: After supper he took another cup of wine and said,

Jesus: This wine is the token of God's new covenant to save you – an agreement sealed with the blood I will pour out for you.

(Luke 22:19–20)

Hebrews 10:1,2,8–10

CAST
Introducer
The Writer to the Hebrews

Introducer: Of the forty references to 'covenant' in the New Testament, half come from one book, the Epistle to the Hebrews. In Chapter 10 the writer sums up the relationship of Jesus to the Old and New Covenants.

The Writer to the Hebrews: The old system in the law of Moses was only a shadow of the things to come, not the reality of the good things Christ has done for us. The sacrifices under the old system were repeated again and again, year after year, but they were never able to provide perfect cleansing for those who came to worship. If they could have provided perfect cleansing, the sacrifices would have stopped, for the worshippers would have been purified once for all time, and their feelings of guilt would have disappeared.

Christ said, 'You did not want animal sacrifices or grain offerings or animals burned on the altar or other offerings for sin, nor were you pleased with them' (though they are required by the law of Moses). Then he added,

'Look, I have come to do your will.' He cancels the first covenant in order to establish the second. And what God wants is for us to be made holy by the sacrifice of the body of Jesus Christ once for all time.

(Hebrews 10:1,2,8–10)

5) POEM BY STEWART HENDERSON

> I've seen them come,
> I've watched them go.
> Inevitably, there are more on the way...
>
> ... Dictators, emperors, maniacs,
> tyrants in formal suits,
> camera adept scoundrels,
> potentates, buffoons,
> wizards, warlocks in uniforms,
> elected sorcerers,
> below average mediums, inaccurate prophets,
> gurus, gargoyles,
> presidents for life, adept philanderers,
> self appointed generals with hailstone armies,
> methodical torturers...
>
> ... And then there were the more personable ones
> who promised you elusive trinkets,
> treasure, pleasure, portfolios of happiness...
> ... It's no wonder I have my weary days.
>
> I have catalogued all such claims,
> brooded over myriad manifestos,
> read reports, repeated names to myself,
> wept and yawned.
>
> How could you?
> How could you have been so gullible?

You put your crosses, waved flags,
sent off your coupons,
worshipped, became cynical and despondent,
to be replaced by the next generation.

And as for those, who with me
laughed at the impertinence of it all,
and met terrible ends,
they are now being suckled in paradise.
There are new arrivals every day.

What I have said I have said.
Love has its laws.
My patience over this is not everlasting.
You have ceased to study my bloodied heart.

6) SERMON

NO GODS BUT GOD

Commandment 1: Exodus 20:1–3 'Then God instructed the people as follows: "I am the LORD your God, who rescued you from slavery in Egypt. Do not worship any other gods besides me."'

INTRODUCTION
This First Commandment is the foundation on which all the other commandments stand. Taken with the preceding verses it sets out the basis of God's covenant agreement with his people of which the Ten Commandments are a part.

Because it is such a foundation stone, it is no accident that Jesus was tempted over this commandment in the wilderness. In Matthew 4:8–10 we read that, as the last of the three tests, the

Devil took Jesus 'to the peak of a very high mountain and showed him the nations of the world and all their glory. "I will give it all to you," he said, "if you will only kneel down and worship me." "Get out of here, Satan," Jesus told him. "For the Scriptures say, 'You must worship the Lord your God; serve only him.'"' If the Devil had broken Jesus here then the failure would have been instant and total.

But what does this commandment mean? Why will God settle only for an exclusive relationship with his people? To understand that we have to look at the whole framework of the Ten Commandments and, in particular, the concept of a covenant.

THE COMMANDMENTS ARE PART OF GOD'S COVENANT
In Alice in Wonderland the Cheshire Cat vanished, leaving only its grin behind. Today we have forgotten so much of the plot of the Old Testament that the Ten Commandments, like the Cheshire Cat's grin, are left hanging unsupported on their own. People tend to imagine that suddenly, without warning, God boomed out the Ten Commandments to the Israelites as a series of unwanted, unsought and arbitrary demands with the threat that if they didn't obey them they would be wiped out.

Now, of course, this is not the case. The commandments were given in a particular time and place and setting, as part of the long relationship of God with the human race and with the Israelites in particular. And we need to comprehend this setting if we are to understand – in any way – either this commandment or the remaining nine.

Part of the problem is that the way the church has handled the Ten Commandments has often been to wrench them out of their context. For instance, it is easy to start listing the commandments with Exodus 20:3: 'Do not worship any other gods besides me'. In fact, the previous two verses are critical. 'Then God instructed the people as follows: "I am the Lord your God, who rescued you from slavery in Egypt."' Without these the First

Commandment – and indeed all the commandments – make little sense.

The key to understanding this commandment, the Ten Commandments and indeed much of the Bible, is in the concept of a covenant. While today the term 'covenant' is most widely used in the sense of making regular payments to a charity it still has a legal meaning of a sealed formal contract between parties. This is close to the meaning in the Bible.

In the world of the Bible the making and keeping of a covenant took a general pattern. A covenant was a solemn and binding agreement between two parties that imposed duties and conditions on both sides. Those conditions generally involved loyalty or obedience. A record of the covenant was kept and there was often some symbol that was a visible reminder to both parties of their treaty to each other. The making of a covenant was also often marked by a sacrificial ritual or a special meal. After the covenant was made, ceremonies might occur regularly where the agreement was renewed or remembered.

The most familiar example to us today of the sort of thing that the Bible would consider a covenant is the traditional marriage ceremony. Here both parties solemnly pledge an exclusive and binding and permanent loyalty to each other in the presence of witnesses. There is an official record, a certificate and wedding rings to act as a symbol of the covenant for both the husband and wife. While there is no element of sacrifice (except for those footing the bill!) no wedding would be a wedding without a meal of some sort. And – as anyone who has ever forgotten a wedding anniversary knows – they are to be regularly remembered.

As the Old Testament Scripture readings showed, the giving of the Ten Commandments fits firmly into the pattern of a covenant. In Exodus we read how God gathered the people together before him (the word covenant has the same origin as the word 'convene'). God said who he was and outlined what he had done for the people of Israel already. Then he announced the covenant and laid down the covenant conditions. The two tablets on which the Ten Commandments were written down acted as both the symbol and the certificate of the covenant. It is likely that the tablets were duplicates of each other and that each bore all the commandments on them. One was God's copy; the other Israel's and both were to be preserved in the box (or ark) of the covenant. The covenant ceremony ended with Moses, Aaron and the other leaders of Israel going up the mountain and eating together in God's presence; an event told briefly in Exodus 24.

The First Commandment and the immediately preceding verses then spell out the very basis of the covenant. Here we see both our side and God's side of the covenant.

GOD'S SIDE OF THE COVENANT: GOD REVEALS HIMSELF

As we saw earlier in the children's talk it is critical that when you make a contract or agreement you know who you are dealing with. It is the same in a covenant.

In these verses we see that God reveals himself to his people. Rather than demanding total and instant obedience, God reminds Israel who he is and what he has done for them.

Who He is

'I am the LORD your God'.

First of all God tells them who it is they are dealing with. For one thing he is God; the one who makes and upholds the universe; he is awesomely powerful and mighty. The people of Israel are being offered a covenant by the one who made everything and who knows everything. Israel could trust God to keep his side of the bargain because he could never be taken by surprise and because he was all-powerful. It was a covenant that they had to agree to. They were going to get no better offer.

And for another thing, he is the LORD. Now contrary to first impressions this word LORD is not just a title. As we mentioned when we considered the commandment to honour God's name, it is a traditional way of representing in English the Hebrew word YHWH which was never written out in its full form and whose precise sound remains uncertain. Although our ancestors thought that this name was pronounced 'Jehovah' it is now believed that 'Yahweh' is more likely. It is the name in which the covenant is made and it acts as the personal name by which the people of Israel could know God. Knowing God's private name gave them access to him. It reflects the sort of idea we allude to in English when we say of someone, 'Oh, I'm on first-name terms with them.'

This name 'the LORD/Yahweh' reminded Israel (and reminds us) that the God of the covenant is a God who we can relate to and know. In fact, the Bible tells us that he is a God who wants to relate to us.

This idea that God is knowable lies behind this First Commandment. The command to worship only God is not given by some remote abstract force or power; it is given by a person who wants an exclusive relationship with us. And as a person (but unlike a force) God can be offended and hurt when we choose not to know him.

What He has done

God however goes further than simply saying 'I am Yahweh your God and you can trust me'. He points out what he has done for the people of Israel already. He says 'I am the LORD your God who rescued you from Egypt'.

Yahweh reminds Israel that he comes to the covenant with a track record. He has saved them in the past. His love is a very concrete and real-life love. Their recent history should have shown the people of Israel that God could be totally trusted. He had shown them that he was a redeeming and rescuing God. He had also shown them in the dramatic events of the Exodus (remember the ten plagues and the crossing of the Red Sea?) that he was more powerful than even the mightiest of the Egyptian gods. Yahweh had shown them that even when 'operating on foreign soil' he was still the very greatest of all gods. Loyalty to him was not going to be a jump in the dark.

So we see that when God comes to strike the covenant

agreement with Israel, he doesn't just demand sole exclusive worship and total obedience. He gives Israel his personal name and reminds them what he has done for them; it is almost as if he is saying to them 'you know me; you can trust me; I have earned the right to have your exclusive trust and obedience'.

God is still like this today. He doesn't demand that we bow before him without showing us what he has done for us first.

THE HUMAN SIDE OF THE COVENANT: GOD EXPECTS A RESPONSE

There are two sides to all agreements, even divine covenants. God first announces his side of the agreement: this, he says, is who I am and this is what I have done for you. He is the creator-redeemer God who cares for his people Israel and has brought them out of slavery. Now, he says, after all I have done for you, this is what I expect from you; this is the response that is appropriate.

The response that the LORD seeks is simple. It is for his people to agree that they will worship him and him alone. It is for them to enter into a relationship with him in which there are to be no third parties. The LORD is looking for a whole hearted response and commitment to his love. He has revealed himself to his people and the condition for him to stay with his people is for them to be totally loyal to him.

We misunderstand the commandments entirely and distort the religion of the Old Testament if we think of these commandments as being conditions that Israel had to meet for God to love her. Rather – as the Bible repeatedly points out – the LORD had loved his people Israel and proved it. These commandments were the guidelines that his people had to keep to stay in the love he had already shed on them. And, like any love relationship, it could be ruined if any other party was brought in to it.

At the heart of the commandments lies the condition that for the LORD to stay as Israel's God and protector they must take him – and him alone – as their only Lord and God.

THE COMMANDMENTS AND THE NEW COVENANT

The First Commandment then is the very basis of the Ten Commandments. In it the LORD reveals himself as a loving, caring God who can be related to and he invites his people to respond to this in absolute loyalty.

Yet despite the enthusiastic acceptance by the people ('We will do everything the LORD has commanded. We will obey!') this commandment – and the covenant – was no sooner made than it was broken. We read at the end of Exodus 24 how God summoned Moses higher up the mountain for more instruction over the course of forty days and forty nights. But even as Moses was receiving details of how the LORD was to be worshipped, the people he had left behind were making the idol of the Golden Calf! And the rest of the history of the Old Testament shows that, despite periods when their religion was more or less pure, the people of Israel continued to hanker after other gods. They saw the exclusive covenant relationship that the LORD wanted with them to be a sort of spiritually open marriage into which anything could be invited. It was only by God's grace that the covenant persisted at all.

Many of their prophets grieved over the failure of Israel to keep the covenant. Jeremiah's prophecy of a new covenant that could be kept must have struck a chord with many people.

With Jesus the promised new covenant became a reality. It was spelt out to his disciples, not on a mountain but in the upper room on the night before his death. Here Jesus announced that the God's dealings with his people were now changing. There was to be a new covenant sealed in his own blood, blood that was to be shed for his followers. Here around the table some of the great covenant themes return; there is a ritual meal, there are instructions to remember (John 13:34: 'So now I am giving you a new commandment: Love each other'), there are symbols (the bread and the wine) and the instructions to remember the covenant ('do this in remembrance of me').

Yet although the covenant has changed some of the conditions stay the same. Under the New Covenant, we are to still love God exclusively. We are to put him before not just idols, but also our ambitions, interests and even our families. In some ways the demands of the New Covenant are harder than those of the old. We must keep the commandments not just externally in what we do but also internally in what we think and say.

But in another way the demands are easier too. If we have come to a living faith in God through Jesus Christ then God has put his Spirit in us. We have God's power within us enabling us to fulfill the demands of the law. We now no longer face trying to fulfill the demands of the commandments in our own strength. Now the commandments are not harsh rules; they are the guidelines given by our heavenly Father to show how we should live as his children.

CONCLUSION

We have journeyed inwards through the commandments from the tenth to the first. This first commandment is the core of the commandments; what is here must lie at the foundation of our relationship with God. It is the basis of all the other commandments and unless we keep this commandment then keeping the rest will do little good. Indeed we will not be able to keep them. Only by keeping God central in our lives can we even attempt to keep these other commandments.

Jesus himself made this point very plain when asked about the greatest commandment. 'God is one', he said to the enquirer (Mark 12:29–31), 'and you must love the Lord your God with all your heart, all your soul, all your mind, and all your strength.'

Jesus' statement, which is merely a reemphasis of this commandment, announces the death sentence over all attempts to serve God by our efforts. To keep this commandment is impossible. To worship God completely, totally and permanently is not something that we can do on our own. We need two things; divine strength to carry out this commandment and an assurance of divine forgiveness that when we fail we can be forgiven.

Jesus provides us with both. Through his death, he allows us to become God's children and to receive his Holy Spirit. The

Holy Spirit helps us to worship God as he should be worshipped; at the same time we are assured of God's forgiveness when we do fail.

We need to come to God and acknowledge that we have sinned and that we have failed to keep this commandment. We need to see in Jesus Christ the only one who has ever kept this commandment completely, and go to him for forgiveness and the strength to live out these commandments.

All the commandments – and this one in particular – turn us to the cross of Christ for forgiveness. And at the cross, Christ forgives us and turns us back to these commandments. But now, assured of his forgiveness and equipped by his Spirit, he encourages us to live by them.

Now, under the New Covenant, the commandments are no longer our enemies and no longer stand in judgement against us. Instead they have become our friends and our guides.

7) SUGGESTED PRAYERS

PRAYER OF CONFESSION

O Lord our God, Father, Son and Holy Spirit, One God almighty, all glorious, we acknowledge before you that we have failed to worship you adequately. We have failed to love you with all our heart, all our soul, all our mind and all our strength. We have broken the covenant you have made by our words, deeds and thoughts. We have put before you the gods of our world; our careers, our wealth and all that we are and want to be.

We acknowledge our sin and in repentance we seek your forgiveness. We ask that you cleanse our hearts through Jesus Christ and pour out your Spirit upon us.

Have mercy on us we pray, through Jesus Christ our lord, Amen.

PRAYER OF COMMITMENT

Lord God, we turn to you now and ask that we will let you become the Lord and the only Lord of our lives. Enable us through your Holy Spirit to know you as the Lord of what we say, what we do, what we think and what we are. Help us to turn from all other gods and to worship you and you alone.

We thank you for your new covenant that you have made for us through Jesus Christ. We praise you and thank you that in him we have a hope that we could never have had otherwise. Thank you for his fulfilment of the law and for the forgiveness of his people that his death brings us.

Thank you too for the fact that the Lord Jesus Christ has risen from the dead and now lives to intercede for us. We thank you for the Holy Spirit who has been given to your New Covenant people, the Church, and who dwells in all those who have come to be your children through the shed blood of Jesus Christ.

Help us Lord, to keep these commandments through the power of your Spirit. Uphold us when we stumble and forgive us when we fall. Help us from this day on to live our lives in single-minded devotion to you, Father, Son and Holy Spirit. For we ask all these things through Jesus Christ our Lord, Amen.

Biography

J.John is widely regarded as one of the most creative Christian speakers in the UK. His much-loved art of storytelling helps us discover God and spiritual meaning – in a way that makes more sense, too, of everyday life.

He is Killy's husband, and father to Michael, Simeon and Benjamin. He loves God and his family, and enjoys food, films and fun.

He lives in Chorleywood, Hertfordshire.

If you would like to know more about the ministry of J.John, or order books and resources, please contact:

The Philo Trust
141 High Street
Rickmansworth
WD3 1AR
United Kingdom

admin@philotrust.com

or visit the website at www.philotrust.com

The Philo Trust is the charity which supports the ministry of J.John. The word *philo* is Greek for brotherly love.

The Philo Trust was launched as a registered charity in 1980. Since then it has enabled J.John to lead nearly 200 missions throughout the UK and overseas, developing many innovative approaches to communicating the message of Christianity.

J.John is also a prolific writer, currently having 14 titles in print in 13 languages.